Terry Pratchett's
Lords and Ladies
Adapted for the stage by

Irana Brown

Samuel French — London
www.samuelfrench-london.co.uk

LORDS AND LADIES

First presented at the Winton Studio Theatre on 13th September 1995 with the following cast:

Young Esme/Granny Weatherwax	Sarah Salholm
Nanny Ogg	Claire March
Magrat Garlick	Irana Brown
King Verence/Baker	Eddie Nias
Young Ridcully/Mustrum Ridcully/Pewsey Ogg	
	Simon Nock
The Bursar	Daniel Morrish
Ponder Stibbons/Thatcher	Allen Stroud
The Librarian	Helena Ward
Casanunda	Tim Keenan
Queen of the Elves/Millie Chillum/Troll	
	Caroline Benger
The Long Man/Lord Lankin	Alan Simpson
Jason Ogg	Stephen Buckmaster
Shawn Ogg/Bestiality Carter	David Salholm
Obidiah/Perdita/Mrs Scorbic	Bryher Mason
Weaver/Elf 6	Caroline Male
Diamanda	Jenny Way
Amanita/Elf 1	Marie Nock (neé Evans)
Elf 2	Vanessa Mansbridge
Elf 3/Coachman	Georgie Thorne
Elf 4	Emma Brown
Elf 5/Mr Spriggins	Neil Girling

Directed by Irana Brown and Sarah Salholm
Designed by Irana Brown, Sarah Salholm and Derek Ware

CAST

Granny Weatherwax, a witch
Nanny Ogg, a witch
Magrat Garlick, former witch, and future queen of Lancre
Verence, King of Lancre
Mustrum Ridcully, Archancellor of the Unseen University
The Bursar, a wizard
Ponder Stibbons, a wizard
The Librarian, an orangutan, and wizard
Casanunda, the world's second greatest lover, a dwarf
Queen of the Elves
The **Long Man**
Jason Ogg, a smith and Morris Man
Shawn Ogg, his brother
Pewsey Ogg, an infant
Bestiality Carter, a comic artisan
Obidiah, the same
Weaver, the thatcher
Thatcher, the weaver
Baker, the tailor
"Diamanda" Tockley
"Perdita" Nitt
"Amanita" Frottidge
Lord Lankin, an elf
Millie Chillum
Mrs Scorbic, a cook
Mr Spriggins, a butler
Coachman
Troll, a troll
Young Esme, Granny Weatherwax as a girl
Young Ridcully, Mustrum Ridcully as a boy
Plus various **elves**, **guests** and **villagers**

ADAPTER'S NOTE

If you are already a fan of Terry Pratchett you will, no doubt, be familiar with the following; in fact you probably know more than me. If not, read on ...

Great A'Tuin, the sky turtle swims through space. On his back stand four elephants, who support the Discworld on their backs. This is a flat world, where the field of magic is strong and the line between belief and fantasy is weak. A fantasy world where witches, wizards, trolls and other fantasy figures find themselves in situations similar to those on our world.

Lords and Ladies is the third novel in the "witches" series of books which feature the popular characters Granny Weatherwax and Nanny Ogg. The action takes place after *Wyrd Sisters* and *Witches Abroad* and before *Maskerade* and *Carpe Jugulum*. Having travelled to Genua to battle her wicked younger sister, Granny Weatherwax and her coven return to Lancre to find an old enemy has returned. In a series of adventures not dissimilar to those of *A Midsummer Night's Dream*, the witches find themselves pitted against the forces of belief and glamour.

NOTES ON MUSIC AND SOUND EFFECTS

One of the themes of **LORDS AND LADIES** concerns the plot and influence of folk songs. Many of the characters find themselves in situations reminiscent of the plots documented in folk songs, in particular the theme of elves stealing into this world and carrying off children and people, and of the human maiden having to fight the Fairy Queen to win the return of her lover.

In our production, we used many different folk songs to cover scene changes. Some of these are listed here; others have not been included as these are not readily available on CD.

We also used several traditional songs to be sung live. Most importantly in ACT II Scene 11, the Rude Mechanicals enter singing a drunken song. We used our own version of The Blackbird Song (which you can find on *The Best of the Wurzels*), but other country songs could work just as well, and there are many good examples on *Folk Music of England* by The Yetties.

One more sound effect which is vital to the script is the Magic Effect/Elf Thrum used in ACT I SCENE 5; ACT I SCENE 9 and lastly in ACT II SCENE 11 which indicates Granny's time/space displacement, and the threat of the elves which only she is mentally aware of. We used a low thrumming noise (a discordant chord on a keyboard) to indicate this.

Of course, it is up to you, as the Director, to choose whether you want to use music, and, if so, what you will use.

The songs of which recordings are readily available are:

Long Lankin: Steeleye Span: *The Best of Steeleye Span*, produced by Chrysalis

The Man with No Name: *Great Western Movie Themes; A Fistful of Dollars*, produced by Laserlight

No, Sir, No: The Yetties: *Folk Music of England*, produced Grasmere Music Ltd

Never Wed an Old Man: Sean O'Neill Band, *Favourite Irish Drinking Songs* produced by Emporio EMPRCD520. (Trad.O'Neill. Erin Music)

Irana Brown

Other Terry Pratchett adaptations
published by Samuel French Ltd

Carpe Jugulum (adapted by Stephen Briggs)
Maskerade (adapted by Stephen Briggs)

ACT I

The stage is split into three levels. UR *and* UL *are two rostra; a flight of steps from each rostrum leads to a balcony above. Between the two rostra is a wooden castle door. The balcony has a stone bridge on it, set back so that there are acting areas in front of it and behind*

When the play begins, the main stage is occupied by the Dancers, an eight-stone circle. The balcony represents Lancre Castle

The stage is in darkness. There is a low thrum, and a refrain of "elf music" is heard; it plays beneath the following dialogue. The Lights come up on the circle

During the following, King Verence enters on to the balcony, as yet unlit

Young Esme (Granny Weatherwax as a girl) runs across the stage, followed by young Ridcully (Mustrum Ridcully as a boy). They exit

Elves appear in the stone circle, looking menacingly outwards

Elves   Elves are wonderful. They provoke wonder.
Elves are marvellous. They cause marvels.
Elves are fantastic. They create fantasies.
Elves are glamorous. They project glamour.
Elves are enchanting. They weave enchantment.
Elves are terrific. They beget terror.

The Lights come up on the whole of the stage

   Young Esme runs on and approaches the circle

Young Esme I'm here. Show me.

   The Queen of the Elves appears in the circle

So you're real, then.

Queen Of course. What's your name, girl?

Young Esme Esmerelda.

Queen And what do you want?

Young Esme I don't want anything. I just wanted to find out if you was real.

Queen To you, certainly. You have good sight. And now you have learned this, what is it you really want? Last week you went all the way up to the mountains above Copperhead to talk to the trolls. What did you want from them?

Young Esme I — wanted to talk to them. D'you know they think time goes backwards? Because you can see the past, they say, and —

Queen (*laughing*) But they are like stupid dwarfs! All they are interested in is pebbles. There is nothing of interest in pebbles.

Young Esme Why can't you come out from between the stones?

Queen I can help you find far more than pebbles.

Young Esme You can't come out of the circle, can you?

Queen Let me give you what you want.

Young Esme I can go anywhere, but you're stuck in the circle. When I am a witch I shall be able to go anywhere.

Queen But you'll never be a witch. They say you won't listen. They say you have no discipline.

Young Esme Oh, you know that, do you? I mean to be a witch whatever they say. You can find things out for yourself. You don't have to listen to a lot of daft old ladies who've never had a life. And, circle lady, I shall be the best witch there has ever been.

Queen With my help I believe you may. Your young man is looking for you.

Young Esme (*shrugging*) I will, will I?

Queen You could be a great witch. You could be anything. Anything you want. Come into the circle.

Young Esme But I'm learning a lot …

Queen Step through the stones now!

Young Esme How do I know … ?

Queen Circle time is nearly over. Think of what you can learn! Now! Step through!

Black-out

Esme and all the Elves except Elf 1 leave the stage. The Queen and Elf 1 are joined by Lankin

The Lights come up on the balcony

Shawn Ogg and Magrat enter. Shawn has a bugle with him

Shawn Meeeyisss Magraaat Garrrrrli-ick! (*He blows a fanfare, continuing through the following*)

Verence Oh hallo. All back safe then?

Magrat Um …

Verence I've really been getting interested in agricultural improvement and soil efficiency. We'll really have to get cracking on this new three-field system.

Magrat But I think we've only got three fields and there isn't much soil in …

Verence It's very important to maintain the correct relationship between grains, legumes and roots. Also I'm seriously considering clover. Shawn, will you stop blowing that damn trumpet!

Shawn But I'm doin' a fanfare, your majesty.

Verence Yes, yes, but you're not supposed to go on. A few notes are sufficient. (*He gestures Shawn away*)

Shawn exits

That's better. Where were we?

Magrat Legumes, I think, but I really came to ——

Verence It all comes down to the soil. Get the soil right, and everything else follows. Incidentally, I'm arranging the marriage for Midsummer Day. I thought you'd like that. I've had some invitations sent out already, to the more obvious guests. And I thought it might be a nice idea to have some sort of fair beforehand. I asked Boggis in Ankh-Morpork to send up their best dressmaker and one of the maids is about your size, and I think you'll be pleased with the result. And my brother and Mr Vitoller's men can't come because they're touring Klatch, but Hwel the playsmith has written a special play for the wedding entertainment. So that's all settled, then?

Magrat Aren't you supposed to ask me?

Verence What ? Um. No, actually. No, kings don't ask. I looked it up. I'm the king, you see, and you are, no offence meant, a subject. I don't have to ask.

There is a pause

Is is the witching? You don't have to give that up entirely, of course. You can be a witchqueen, although I think that means you have to wear rather revealing clothes and keep cats and give people poisoned apples. I read that somewhere.

Magrat No, it's not that — um …

Verence You're not upset, are you?

Magrat What? Oh. No. Me? No.

Verence Good. That's all sorted out, then.
Magrat Um …
Verence We're doing some marvellous things with legumes. Scientific husbandry. Come and look at this.
Magrat Where are we going?
Verence The old rose garden.

The Lights go down on the balcony and up on the Dancers, where the Queen of the Elves, Lankin and Elf 1 are gathered

Magrat and Verence exit

Queen And this time there will be no defeat. The land will welcome us. It must hate humans now.
Elf 1 But there were witches. I remember the witches.
Queen Once, yes. But now: poor things, poor things. Scarce any power in them at all. And suggestible pliant minds. Leave the witches to me.
Lankin I remember the witches. Minds — like metal.
Queen Not any more. I tell you, leave them to me! And then you can have them. For me, I rather fancy a mortal husband. A union of the worlds. To show them that this time we mean to stay.
Lankin The king won't like that.
Queen And when has that ever mattered? The time is right, Lankin. The circles are opening. Soon we can return.
Elf 1 And I can hunt again. When? When?
Queen Soon.

Music plays; an excerpt from "Long Lankin"

Black-out

SCENE 1

The Dancers

The main stage is lit

The music fades

The three witches, Granny Weatherwax, Nanny Ogg and Magrat Garlick enter, each from a different stage entrance, each with a broomstick

Granny In the middle of my bloody herbs!

Magrat On the palace garden!
Nanny Poor little mite! And he was holding it up to show me too!

There is a pause

Granny What are you talking about Gytha Ogg?
Nanny Our Pewsey was growing mustard and cress on a flannel for his Nan.
He shows it to me and just as I bends down — splat! Crop circle!
Granny This is serious. It's been years since they've been as bad as this.
We all know what it means. What we've got to do now is —
Magrat I don't know what it means. I mean Old Goodie Whemper —
Granny ⎫
Nanny ⎬ (*together*) Maysherestinpeace.
Magrat — told me once that the circles were dangerous, but she never
said anything about why.
Granny Never told you about the Dancers?
Nanny Never told you about the Long Man?
Magrat What Dancers? You mean the old stones?
Granny All you need to know right now is that we've got to put a stop
to Them.
Magrat What Them?
Granny The circles, of course.
Magrat Oh no. I can tell by the way you said it. You said Them as though
it was some sort of curse. It wasn't just a them, it was a them with a
capital the. And who's the Long Man?
Granny We do not ever talk about the Long Man.
Nanny No harm in telling her about the Dancers, at any rate.
Granny Yes, but … You know … I mean … She's Magrat.
Magrat What's that meant to mean?
Granny You probably won't feel the same about Them, is what I am
saying. Mind you, a circle might not find the Dancers. We can always
hope. Could be just random.
Nanny But if one opens up inside the —
Magrat You do this on purpose! You talk in code the whole time! But
you won't be able to when I'm queen!
Nanny Oh? Young Verence popped the question then?
Magrat Yes!
Granny (*icily*) When's the happy event?
Magrat Two weeks' time. Midsummer Day.
Nanny Bad choice. Shortest night o' the year …
Granny Gytha Ogg!
Magrat And you'll be my subjects. And you'll have to curtsy and
everything!

Granny We will, will we?

Magrat Yes, and if you don't you can get thrown in prison.

Granny My word. Dearie, dearie me. I wouldn't like that. I wouldn't like that at all.

Nanny Queen Magrat, eh? Well, the old castle could do with a bit of lightening up ...

Granny Oh, it'll lighten up all right.

Magrat Well, anyway, I don't have to bother with this sort of thing. Whatever it is. It's your business. I shan't have time, I'm sure.

Granny I'm sure you can please yourself, your going-to-be majesty.

Magrat Hah! I can! You can jol... you can damn' well find another witch for Lancre! Another soppy girl to do all the dreary work and never be told anything and be talked over the head of the whole time. I've got better things to do.

Granny Better things than being a witch?

Magrat Yes!

Nanny Oh dear.

Granny Oh well, then I expect you'll be wanting to be off. Back to your palace I'll be bound.

Magrat picks up her broomstick

(*Grabbing the broomstick handle*) Oh, no you don't. Queens ride around in golden coaches and whatnot. Each to their own. Brooms is for witches.

Nanny Now come on you two. Someone can be a queen and a w ——

Magrat Who cares? (*She drops the broomstick*) I don't have to bother with that sort of thing any more.

Magrat exits

Nanny You daft old besom, Esme. Just because she's getting wed.

Granny You know what she'd say if we told her. The Gentry. Circles. She'd say it was — nice. Best for her if she's out of it. I might have to go borrowing.

Nanny Why?

Granny To see what's happening, of course! If only I could do it with bees. Hives notice changes in the land.

Nanny Now Esme, you know no-one's ever been able to do it with bees, not even Black Aliss. They ain't been active for years and years. We ought to have kept 'em cleared.

Granny True. There's been things going on. All the bracken and weeds is trampled around the stones. I reckon someone's been dancing.

Nanny They never.

Granny They have. I'm going to get to the bottom of this.
Nanny Who'd be daft enough to dance round the stones?
Granny We shall have to find out.

Granny exits

Black-out

A chorus of a folk song is sung backstage

SCENE 2

Nanny's house; Lancre Smithy

A small oven represents the forge. It has an old iron kettle and some teacups on top

The main stage is lit

Jason Ogg and the Rude Mechanicals are on stage

The song ends

Nanny enters

The Rude Mechanicals shuffle off

Nanny Jason Ogg, I wants a word with you.
Jason I got to this do bit of brazing for old ——
Nanny So, what's been happening in these parts while we've been away, my lad?
Jason Oh, well, us had a big whirlwind on Hogwatchnight and one of Mother Peason's hens laid the same egg three times, and old Poorchick's cow gave birth to a seven-headed snake — and there ——
Nanny Been pretty normal, then.
Jason All very quiet, really.

Nanny takes a step towards Jason, who backs away

Nanny I'll find out sooner or later, you know ... (*She takes another step*) I always does, you know ... (*One more step*) You know you always feels better for telling your old mum.
Jason Weren't my fault, Mum! How could I stop 'em?

Nanny What them would these be, my son?
Jason That young Diamanda and that Perdita and that girl with the red hair from over in Bad Ass. I says to old Peason, I says you'd have something to say, I tole 'em Mistress Weatherwax'd get her knic ... would definitely be sarcastic when she found out. But they just laughs. They said they could teach 'emselves witching.
Nanny Diamanda? Don't recall the name.
Jason Really she's Lucy Tockley. She says Diamanda is more — witchy.
Nanny Ah. The one that wears the big floppy felt hat? (*She makes a pot of tea during the following*)
Jason Yes, Mum.
Nanny She's the one that paints her nails black, too?
Jason Yes, Mum.
Nanny Old Tockley sent her off to school, didn't he?
Jason Yes, Mum. She came back while you was gone.
Nanny Ah. Floppy hat and black nails and education. Oh, dear. How many gels are there?
Jason 'Bout half a dozen. But they'm good at it, Mum. And it ain't as if they've been doing anything bad. And I knows you've always said there weren't enough girls interested in learnin' witching. They goes up and dances up in the mountains every full moon. People do say that they dances in the altogether.
Nanny Altogether what?
Jason You know, Mum. In the nudd.
Nanny Cor. There's a thing. Anyone see where they go?
Jason Nah. Weaver the thatcher says they always gives him the slip.

Granny Weatherwax enters unsteadily with an 'I ATE'NT DEAD' sign around her neck. She sits down

Nanny (*handing Granny a cup of tea*) Cup of tea.
Granny Good job, too. Mouth tastes of moths.
Nanny Thought you did owls at night?
Granny Yeah, but you ends up for days trying to twist your head right round. At least bats always face the same way. Half a dozen people have been going up there. Every full moon! Gels, by the shape of them. You only see silhouettes, with bats.
Nanny (*carefully*) You done well there. Girls from round here, you reckon?
Granny Got to be. They ain't using broomsticks.
Nanny (*sighing*) There's Agnes Nitt, old Threepenny's daughter. And the Tockley girl. And some others. I asked our Jason. Sorry.

Jason takes a look at Granny's face and exits rapidly

Granny I'm a silly old fool, ain't I?

Nanny No, no. Borrowing's a real skill. You're really good at it.

Granny Prideful, that's what I am. Once upon a time I'd of thought of asking people, too, instead of fooling around being a bat.

Nanny Our Jason wouldn't have told you. He only told me 'cos I would've made his life a living hell if he didn't. That's what a mother's for.

Granny I'm losing my touch, that's what it is. Getting old. Supposing Magrat'd been here. She'd see me being daft.

Nanny Well. She's safe in the castle. Learning how to be queen. S'funny, royalty. It's like magic. You take some girl with a bum like two pigs in a blanket and a head full of air and she marries a king or prince or someone and suddenly she's this radiant, right royal princess.

Granny Old Tockley's girl?

Nanny That's right.

Granny Come on — we ain't got much time. It's not just the girls. There's something out there too. Some kind of mind movin' around. The Lords and Ladies are trying to find a way. They always used to say something can come through if something goes the other way …

Nanny Ain't you scared?

Granny No. But I hope they are.

Nanny Ooo, it's true what they say. You're a prideful one, Esmerelda Weatherwax.

Granny Who says that?

Nanny Well, you did. Just now.

Granny I wasn't feeling well.

Black-out

SCENE 3

Diamanda's house

There is a small table with a lit candle on it on stage. There is also a chalk circle of magical symbols on the floor

The main stage is lit

The young coven — Diamanda, Perdita and Amanita — are on stage, sitting within the circle. Diamanda is showing the others tarot cards

Diamanda (*coldly*) Are you paying attention, sister?

Perdita Yes, Diamanda.

Diamanda This is the Moon for those who weren't paying attention. And what do we see here, you Amanita?

Amanita Um ... It's got a picture of the moon on it?
Diamanda Of course it's not the moon. It's a non-mimetic convention, not tied to a conventional referencing system, actually.
Amanita Ah.

Granny and Nanny enter suddenly through the central door

Granny Blessings be upon this house.
Nanny 'Ere, you're doing that wrong. You don't want to muck about with a hand like that. You've got a double onion there. What's all the chalk on the floor? And heathen writing. Not that I've got anything against heathens. I'm practically one but I don't write on the floor. You'll never get the chalk out.
Perdita Um, it's a magic circle. Um, hallo, Mrs Ogg. Um. It's to keep bad influences away.
Granny Tell me, my dear. Do you think it's working?
Diamanda Who's this?
Perdita Um, it's Granny Weatherwax. Um, she's a witch, um —
Diamanda What level?
Granny Levels, eh? Well, I suppose I'm level one.
Diamanda Just starting?
Nanny (*to Perdita*) Oh dear. Tell you what, if we was to turn the table over we could probably hide behind it, no problem.
Granny Oh, yes. Just starting. Every day, just starting.
Diamanda You stupid old woman you don't frighten me. I know all about the way you old ones frighten superstitious peasants, actually. Muttering and squinting. It's not real witchcraft.
Nanny I'll — er — I'll just go into the scullery and — er — see if I can fill any buckets with water, shall I? (*During the following, she takes off her witch's hat and chews the brim*)
Granny I 'spect you'd know all about witchcraft, I 'spect you're really good at it.
Diamanda Quite good.
Granny Show me. I learned my craft from Nanny Gripes who learned it from Goody Heggty, who got it from Nana Plumb, who was taught it by Black Aliss, who ...
Diamanda So what you're saying is that no-one has actually learned anything new?

There is a pause

Nanny Bugger, I've bitten right through the brim. Right through.
Granny I see.

Nanny Look, right through the lining and everything. Two dollars and curing his pig that hat cost me. That's two dollars and a pig cure I shan't see again in a hurry.

Diamanda So you can just go away old woman.

Granny But we ought to meet again. How about noon?

The "Man With No Name" theme from "The Good, the Bad and the Ugly" plays

Diamanda Certainly. What are we fighting for?

Granny Fighting? We ain't fighting. We're just showing each other what we can do. Friendly like. I'd better be goin'. Us old people need our sleep, you know how it is.

Diamanda And what does the winner get?

Granny Oh, the winner gets to win. Don't bother to see us out. You didn't see us in.

Black-out

SCENE 4

Lancre Castle

A screen stands on the stage

The main stage is lit

Magrat is on stage wearing a nightgown

Millie Chillum enters carrying a large bundle of clothing and a diagram

Magrat Millie Chillum?

Millie (*curtsying and staying down*) Yes'm?

Magrat It's me, Magrat. Hallo.

Millie (*still curtsying*) Yes'm.

Magrat What's up with you, Millie?

Millie Yes'm. (*She curtsies twice*)

Magrat I said it's me. You don't have to look at me like that.

Millie (*curtsying*) Yes 'm.

Magrat If you say "Yes 'm" again, it will go hard with you.

Millie (*curtsying*) Ye … right, your majesty, m'm.

Magrat I'm not queen yet, Millie. And you've known me for twenty years.

Millie (*curtsying*) Yes'm. But you're going to be Queen. So me mam told me I was to be respectful.

Magrat Oh. Well. All right then. Where are my clothes?

Millie (*curtsying*) Got 'em here, your pre-majesty.

Magrat They're not mine. And please stop going up and down all the time. I feel a bit sick.

Millie The King ordered 'em from Sto Helit special, m'm.

Magrat and Millie study the clothes and the diagram which shows how to assemble the outfit

Magrat This is a standard queen outfit, then?

Millie Couldn't say, m'm.

Magrat and Millie go behind the screen with the clothes and diagram

Magrat Is this the pantoffle?

Millie I think you've got it up the wrong way, m'm. Which bit's the farthingale?

Magrat Says here insert Tab A into Slot B. Can't find Slot B. These're like saddlebags. I'm not wearing these. And this thing?

Millie A ruff, m'm. Um. They're all the rage in Sto Helit, my brother says.

Magrat You mean they make people angry? And what's this?

Millie Brocade, I think. (*She comes out from behind the screen*)

Shawn Ogg enters

Magrat (*coming out from behind the screen*) It's like cardboard. Do I have to wear this sort of thing every day? Verence just trots around in leather gaiters and an old jacket!

Millie Ah, but you're queen. Queens can't do that sort of thing. It's all right for kings to go wandering around with their arse half out their trouse ... I mean, I mean — I mean queens has got to be ladylike. The King got books about it. Etti-quetty and stuff. It really suits you, your soon-going-to-be-majesty.

Magrat My word. And what happens now? What's the King doing?

Millie Oh, he had breakfast early and buggered off over to Slice to show old Muckbe how to breed his pigs out of a book.

Magrat So what do I do? What's my job?

Millie Dunno, m'm. Reigning I suppose. Walking around in the garden. Holding court. Doin' tapestry. That's very popular among queens. And then — er — later on there's the royal succession.

Magrat Where's everyone gone?

Shawn Everyone's down in the square, miss.

Magrat What's happening in the square, then?

Shawn They say there's a couple of witches having a real set-to, miss.
Magrat What? Not your mother and Granny Weatherwax!
Shawn Oh, no miss. Some new witch.
Magrat I'm going to have a look.
Shawn Oh, I don't think that'd be a good idea, miss.
Magrat We happen to be Queen. Nearly. So you don't tell one one can't do things, or one'll have you cleaning the privies!
Shawn But I does clean the privies. Even the garderobe ——
Magrat And that's going for a start. One's seen it.
Shawn What I meant was you'll have to wait till I've gone down to the armoury to fetch my horn for the fanfare
Magrat One won't need a fanfare, thank you very much. One can blow my own trumpet, thank you.
Shawn Yes, miss.
Magrat Miss what?
Shawn Miss Queen.
Magrat And don't you forget it.

Black-out

SCENE 5

Lancre Square

The main stage is lit

There are benches and chairs on the stage

Nanny — carrying a towel, bucket and plate of oranges — and a crowd are on stage. Among the crowd are young Pewsey Ogg, Nanny's grandson — on the opposite side of the stage from Nanny — and Jason Ogg

"Eye of the Tiger" plays, fading swiftly

Granny enters

The music fades

Granny What's that for?
Nanny Half time. And I done you a plate of oranges. You look as if you could do with eating something, anyway. You don't look as if you've had anything today ... You daft old besom! What've you been doing.
Granny I had to ...

Nanny You've been up at the stones, haven't you! Trying to hold back the Gentry.

Granny Of course. Someone's got to.

There is a sound effect which indicates a sinister presence outside the kingdom

Nanny You all right, Esme?

Granny Fine! I'm fine! Nothing wrong with me, all right?

Nanny Have you had any sleep at all? You haven't, have you? And then you think you can just stroll down here and confound this girl?

Granny I don't know.

Nanny Oh well ... you better sit down here, before you fall down. Suck an orange.

The young coven — Diamanda, Amanita, Perdita — enter and stand on the opposite side of the stage to Nanny and Granny

Granny Look at 'em. All in black again.

Nanny Well, we wear black too.

Granny Only 'cos it's respectable and servicable. Not because it's romantic. Hah! The Lords and Ladies might as well be here already. (*She dozes off during the following*)

Perdita Morning, Mrs Ogg.

Nanny Afternoon, Agnes.

Perdita Um, what happens now?

Nanny Dunno. Up to you, I suppose.

Perdita Diamanda says why does it have to be here and now?

Nanny So's everyone can see. That's the point, ain't it? Nothing hole and corner about it. Everyone's got to know who's the best at witchcraft. Everyone sees the winner win and the loser lose. That way there's no argument, eh?

Perdita Um, what happens to the loser?

Nanny Nothing, really. Generally she leaves the place. You can't be a witch if people've seen you beat.

Perdita Um. I wish this wasn't happening, Mrs Ogg. Diamanda says Mistress Weatherwax has got a very impressive stare, Mrs Ogg. So the test is — just staring, Mrs Ogg.

Nanny You mean the old first-one-to-blink-or-look-away challenge?

Perdita Um ... yes.

Nanny Right. But we'd better do a magic circle first. Don't want anyone else getting hurt, do we?

Perdita Do you mean using Skorkian Runes or the Triple Invocation octogram?

Nanny Never heard of them things, dear. I always does a magic circle like this ... (*She draws a circle with the toe of her boot*)
Perdita That's a magic circle? But you didn't chant or anything.
Nanny No?
Perdita There has to be a chant, doesn't there?
Nanny Dunno. Never done one. I could sing you a comic song if you like?
Perdita Um. No.
Nanny I like your black lace hanky. Very good for not showing the bogies.
Perdita Um. Shall we start, then?

Jason Ogg places two chairs in the circle facing each other

Nanny Right. (*She moves to Granny*) Wake up! All you've got to do is stare her down!
Granny I weren't asleep. I was just resting me eyes. At least she knows the importance of the stare, then. Hah! Who does she think she is? I've been staring at people, all my life!
Nanny Yes, that's what's bothering me ... (*She spots Pewsey Ogg; calling to him*) Aaahhh ... Who's Nana's little boy, then?

Pewsey moves across the stage to Nanny

Pewsey Want sweetie.
Nanny Just a moment, my duck, I'm talking to the lady.
Pewsey Want sweetie now.
Nanny Bugger off, my precious, Nana's busy right this minute.
Pewsey Now sweetie now!
Granny If you don't go away. I will personally rip your head off and fill it with snakes.
Pewsey Funny lady.
Nanny Tell you what — you see them young ladies on the other side of the square? They've got lots of sweeties.

Pewsey moves back across the circle to Diamanda's group

Granny That's germ warfare, that is.
Nanny Come on. Our Jason's put a couple of chairs in the circle.
Perdita Er ... Mrs Ogg? Er ... Diamanda says you don't understand, she says they won't be trying to out-stare one another ... (*She whispers in Nanny's ear, indicating the chairs*)

Nanny whispers in Granny's ear. A whisper goes around the crowd. Granny and Diamanda turn the chairs to face the audience, sit in them and begin to stare at the sky

Pause

Magrat runs on

Magrat What's happening, Nanny?
Nanny Oops, sorry. Didn't hear no fanfare. I'd curtsy only it's my legs.
Magrat What're they doing?
Nanny Staring contest. Bugger that Diamanda girl! She's got Esme trying to outstare the sun. No looking away, no blinking —
Magrat That's terrible!
Nanny It's bloody stupid is what it is. Can't think what's got into Esme. As if power's all there is to witching! She knows that. Witching's not power, it's how you harness it.
Magrat They'll have to stop at sunset.
Nanny Esme won't last till sunset. Look at her. All slumped up.
Magrat I suppose you couldn't use some magic to …
Nanny If Esme found out, she'd kick me round the kingdom. Anyway, the others'd spot it. I cheat for myself. You can't cheat for other people.
Magrat I could have it stopped.
Nanny You'd make an enemy for life.
Magrat I thought Granny was my enemy for life.
Nanny If you think that, my girl, you've got no understanding. One day you'll find out Esme Weatherwax is the best friend you ever had.
Magrat But we've got to do something! Can't you think of anything?

There is a pause. Suddenly Nanny produces a bag of sweets and waves it across the stage at Pewsey. He runs across the square, steps into the magic circle and falls to the floor screaming. Granny looks round and helps him up. Then she takes him to Nanny and resumes her seat. Diamanda does not move

Amanita Diamanda has won! Mistress Weatherwax looked away!
Nanny Oh yes? Pull the other one, it's got bells on. This is not a contest about power, you stupid girls, it is a contest about witchcraft. Do you not even begin to know what being a witch is? Is a witch someone who would look around when she heard a child scream?
Crowd Yes! (*They cheer etc.*)

Diamanda runs off, followed by her coven

Granny lies on a bench with the towel over her face

Granny Gytha? You knows I don't normally touch strong licker, but I've heard you mention the use of brandy for medicinal purposes.
Nanny Coming right up.

Nanny produces a bottle of brandy from her pocket and hands it to Granny

Granny (*to Magrat*) Good-afternoon, your pre-majesty. Come to be gracious at me, have you?

Magrat (*coldly*) Well done. Can one have a word with you, Na ... Mrs Ogg?

Nanny Right you are, your queen.

Magrat You ——

Nanny I know what you're going to say. But there wasn't any danger to the little mite ...

Magrat But you ... ?

Nanny Me? I hardly did anything. They didn't know he was going to run into the circle, did they? They both reacted just like they would normally, didn't they? Fair's fair. No-one cheated ... So you won't be telling anyone you saw me wave the bag of sweets at him, will you?

Magrat No, Nanny.

Nanny There's a good going-to-be-queen.

Magrat Nanny? How did Verence know when we were coming back?

Nanny Couldn't say. Kings are a bit magical, mind. They can cure dandruff and that. Probably woke up one morning and his royal prerogative gave him a tickle. Keeping busy up there, are you?

Magrat One's doing very well, thank you. He knew we were coming back. He'd even got the invitations sorted out. Oh, by the way — there's one for you.

Nanny I know, one got it this morning. Who's Ruservup?

Magrat RSVP. It means you ought to say if you're coming.

Nanny Oh, one'll be along all right, catch one staying away. Has one's Jason sent one his invite yet?

Magrat looks blank

Thought not. Not a skilled man with a pen, our Jason.

Magrat Invitation to what?

Nanny Didn't Verence tell one? It's a special play that's been written special for you.

Magrat Oh yes. The Entertainment.

Nanny Right. It's going to be on Midsummer Eve.

Black-out

The "Twilight Zone" music plays

SCENE 6

Lancre Smithy

The oven sets the scene as before

The main stage is lit. The music stops

*Jason Ogg and the Rude Mechanicals — Bestiality Carter, Obidiah, Weaver,
Thatcher and Baker — are on stage. Bestiality Carter is wearing a dress
and they are all looking at play scripts*

Jason It's got to be special, on Midsummer's Eve.
Carter I feel a right twit. A dress on! I just hope my wife doesn't see
me!
Jason Says here that it's (*he reads*) "A beaut-i-ful story of the love of
the Queen of the Fairies" — that's you, Bestiality ——
Carter Thank you very much.
Jason (*reading*) — "for a mortal man". Plus "A hum-or-rous int-ter-lude
with Comic Artisans" ...
Weaver What's an artisan?
Jason Dunno. Type of well, I reckon. Yeah. They've got 'em down on
the plains. I repaired a pump for one once. Artisan wells.
Weaver What's comic about them?
Jason Maybe people fall down 'em in a funny way?
Obidiah Why can't we do a Morris like normal?
Jason Morris is for every day. We got to do something cultural. This
come all the way from Ankh-Morpork.
Baker We could do the Stick and Bucket Dance.
Jason No-one is to do the Stick and Bucket Dance ever again. Old Mr
Thrum still walks with a limp, and it were three months ago.
Weaver Who's this bugger "Exeunt Omnes"?
Obidiah I don't think much of my part, it's too small.
Weaver It's his poor wife I feel sorry for.
Baker And why's there got to be a lion in it?
Jason 'Cos it's a play! No-one'd want to see it if it had a — a donkey in
it! Oi can just see people comin' to see a play 'cos it had a donkey in it.
This play was written by a real playsmith! Hah, Oi can just see a real
playsmith putting donkeys in a play! Now just you all shut up!
Carter I don't feel like the Queen of the Fairies.
Weaver You'll grow into it.
Jason And you've got to rehearse.
Carter Well I ain't doin' it where anyone else can see. Even if we go out
in the woods somewhere, people'll be bound to see.

Weaver They won't recognize you in your make-up.
Carter Make-up!
Thatcher Yeah, and your wig.
Weaver He's right, though. If we're going to make fools of ourselves, I don't want no-one to see me until we're good at it.
Thatcher Somewhere off the beaten track, like.
Baker Out in the country.
Obidiah Where no-one goes.

Black-out

Scene 7

The road

The main stage is lit

Ridcully, Ponder, the Bursar and the Librarian (an orangutan) are in a coach, with a coachman driving. They all bounce in unison over various bumps in the road

Bursar I spy with my little eye, something beginning with — H.
Librarian Oook.
Bursar No.
Ponder Horizon.
Bursar You guessed!
Ponder Of course I guessed. I'm supposed to guess. We've had S for sky, C for Cabbage, O for — for oook, and there's nothing else.
Bursar I'm not going to play any more if you're going to guess.
Ridcully There'll be lots to see in Lancre. Used to spend whole summers up there. You know — things could have been very different. There was this girl ——
Ponder Pretty, was she, sir?
Ridcully No. No, I can't say she was. Striking . That's the word. Tall. Hair so blond it was nearly white. And eyes like gimlets, I tell you.
Ponder You don't mean that dwarf who runs the delicatessen in ——
Ridcully I mean you always got the impression she could see right through you. And she could run ... I would have married her, you know ... What a summer. Very like this one really. Crop circles were bursting like raindrops. I'd have given it all up for her. Every blasted octogram and magic spell. Without a second thought.
Ponder So what happened sir?
Ridcully Oh, she turned me down. Said there were things she wanted to do. Said there'd be time enough. Term started. Wrote her a lot of letters

but she never answered 'em. Probably never got 'em, they probably eat the mail up there. Never did go back. Exams and so on. Expect she's dead now, or some fat old granny with a dozen kids. Would've wed her like a shot. Hah — just wish I could remember her name.

Casanunda enters, carrying a stepladder and a crossbow. He threatens the Coachman with the crossbow

Casanunda Kneel and deliver!
Ridcully What's that?
Ponder I think it's a very small highwayman.
Casanunda I do apologize for this. I find myself a little short.
Coachman You little bastard. I'm going to knock your block off. What's that on your back? A hump?
Casanunda Ah, you've noticed the stepladder. Let me demonstrate.

Casanunda climbs up the ladder to the Coachman and knocks him into the road

Ponder A dwarf has just climbed up a small stepladder and kicked the coachman into the middle of the road. Now he's coming towards us.
Ridcully Oh good.
Casanunda Your money, or I'm sorry to say your — —

Ridcully points his fingertips to Casanunda's L and there is an explosion

I wonder if I might be allowed to rephrase my demands? My card.
Ridcully "Giamo Casanunda — World's second greatest Lover." Are you really an outrageous liar?
Casanunda No.
Ridcully Why are you trying to rob coaches then?
Casanunda I am afraid I was waylaid by bandits.
Ridcully But it says here that you are a fine swordsman.
Casanunda I was outnumbered.
Ridcully Hop in.
Casanunda Is that an ape asleep in there?
Ponder Yes. Hadn't you better apologize to the coachman?
Casanunda No, but I could kick him again harder if he likes.
Ridcully And that's the Bursar. Hey Bursar? Bursssaaarrr! No, he's out like a light. Just push him under the seat. Can you play Cripple Mr Onion?
Casanunda Not very well.
Ridcully Capital!

There is a pause. The coach travels on

*Ridcully and Casanunda play "Cripple Mr Onion"; Ponder and the
Librarian watch. The Bursar remains unconscious. Casanunda wins
several hands. Ridcully throws down his cards*

Casanunda But I put it on my visiting card: "Outrageous liar". Right there.
Ridcully Yes, but I thought you were lying!

Ridcully produces a bag of money and hands it to Casanunda

Casanunda Hmm. You don't have "outrageous liar" on your visiting
card, by any chance?
Ridcully No!
Casanunda It's just that I can recognize chocolate money when I see it.
Ridcully Now that, Mr Stibbons, is logical thought. You could learn a lot
from this man. He doesn't go on about parasite universes all the time.
Ponder Parallel!
Ridcully Which ones are the parasite ones, then?
Ponder There aren't any! Parallel universes, I said. Universes where
things didn't happen like ... Well, you know that girl you wanted to
marry? Well — in a way, you did marry her.
Ridcully Nope. Pretty certain I didn't. You remember that sort of thing.
Ponder Ah, but not in this universe ...
Ridcully You suggestin' I nipped into some other universe to get married?
Ponder No! I mean, you got married in that universe and not in this
universe.
Ridcully Did I? What? A proper ceremony and everything? Hmm. You
sure?
Ponder Certain, Archancellor.
Ridcully My word! I never knew that. So why don't I remember it?
Ponder Because the you in the other universe is different from the you
here. It was a different you that got married. He's probably settled down
somewhere. He's probably a great-grandad by now.
Ridcully He never writes, I know that. And the bastard never invited
me to the wedding.
Ponder Who?
Ridcully Him.
Ponder But he's you!
Ridcully Is he? Huh! You'd think I'd think of me, wouldn't you? What
a bastard.

Black-out

SCENE 8

The Dancers

The main stage is lit

Granny is hiding behind a stone

Diamanda runs on

Granny (*stepping out*) Evenin' miss.

Diamanda You? You did follow me. So you're hunting me now?

Granny No. I was just waiting. I knew you'd come up here. You haven't got anywhere else to go. You've come to call her, haven't you? Let me tell you something about beautiful women in red with stars in their hair. She offered you lots of power, I expect. All you wanted. For free. Because it happened before. There's always someone who'll listen. When you're lonely, and the people around you seem too stupid for words, and the world is full of secrets no-one'll tell you ...

Diamanda Are you reading my mind?

Granny Yours? Hah! Flowers and suchlike. Dancing about without your drawers on. Mucking about with cards and bits of string. And it worked, I expect. She gave you power, for a while. Oh, she must have laughed. And then there is less power and more price. And then there is no power, and you're payin' every day. They always take more than they give. And what they give has less than no value. And they end up taking everything. What they get from us is our fear. What they want from us, most of all, is our belief. If you call them, they will come. You'll give them a channel if you call them here, at circle time, where the world's thin enough to hear. The power in the dancers is weak enough as it is. And I'm not having the — Lords and Ladies back.

Diamanda You mad old woman, you've got it all wrong! Elves aren't like that ...

Granny Don't say the word. They come when called.

Diamanda Good! Elf, elf, elf! Elf ...

Granny slaps Diamanda

Granny Even you know that's stupid and childish. If you stay here, there's to be none of this stuff any more. Or you can go somewhere else and find a future, be a great lady, you've got the mind for it. But if you stay here and keep trying to call the — Lords and Ladies, you'll be up against me again. Not playing stupid games in the daylight, but real witchcraft. You don't know nothin' about that. And it don't allow for mercy.

Diamanda Go?

Diamanda runs between the stones and disappears

Granny You stupid child! Not that way! Oh, drat.

Granny runs into the circle after Diamanda

There is a "magical" sound effect and the noise of metal being torn away; the Lights flicker

Black-out

Five of the stones are removed; the object is to make it look as if we are on the other side of the ring

The Queen of the Elves and her followers enter

The Lights come up

Granny and Diamanda appear, running through the stones from US

Queen Kneel before your Queen, you.
Granny Shan't. Won't.
Queen You are in my kingdom, woman. You do not come or go without the leave of me. You will kneel!
Granny I come and go without the leave of anyone . Never done it before, ain't starting now. (*To Diamanda*) These are your elves. Beautiful, ain't they? The only reason we're still alive now is that we're more fun alive than dead.
Queen You know you shouldn't listen to the crabbed old woman. What can she offer?
Granny More than snow in the summer time. Look at their eyes.
Queen Take my hand, child. Get out of her mind, old crone.
Granny I ain't in her mind, elf. I'm keeping you out.
Queen You have some power. Amazing. I never thought you'd amount to anything, Esmerelda Weatherwax. But it's no good here. Kill them both. But not at the same time. Let the other one watch.

The Queen exits

Two Elves approach Granny and Diamanda and draw their daggers

Granny When the time comes, run.

Diamanda What time?

Granny You'll know. Oh, dearie me, oh spare my life, I am but a poor old woman and skinny also. Oh spare my life, young sir. Oh, lawks. (*She falls on her knees and sobs*)

Elf 1 hauls Granny up by her shoulders; she punches him in the groin. Diamanda runs away. Granny elbows Elf 2 and runs after Diamanda. The Elves laugh and pursue

Granny Head for the gap between the Piper and the Drummer!

Diamanda Which ones are they?

Granny You don't even know that?

Granny and Diamanda exit R, followed by the Elves. Granny and Diamanda re-enter L

Two Elves with bows and arrows appear on the balcony and fire arrows down on to the stage

Diamanda is hit and falls to the floor

Granny picks Diamanda up and runs into the stone circle

There is a "magical" sound effect and the Lights flicker

Black-out

The five stones previously removed from the circle are returned; we are now back where the scene started

Nanny enters carrying a frying-pan and hides behind a stone

The Lights come up

Granny, Diamanda and Elf 1 appear out of the circle. The elf raises its dagger

Nanny Ogg appears and floors the elf with the frying-pan

Nanny Cor, it doesn't half whiff, don't it? You can smell elves a mile off.

Granny (*dropping Diamanda*) Elf shot. The point's still in there.

Nanny Oh, bugger. I could probably get the point out, no problem, but I don't know about the poison. (*She produces a penknife from her dress and waves it threateningly at the elf*)

Granny What the hell are you doing?

Nanny Going to put it out of its misery, Esme.

Granny Doesn't look miserable to me.

Nanny Could soon arrange that, Esme.

Granny Don't go torturing it just because it's lying down, Gytha.

Nanny Damn well ain't waiting for it to stand up again, Esme.

Granny Gytha!

Nanny Well, they used to carry off babbies. I ain't having that again. The thought of someone carrying off our Pewsey …

Granny Even elves ain't that daft. Never seen such a sticky child in all my life. Come on, I'll carry her, you bring Mr Tinkerbell.

Nanny That was brave of you, carrying her over your shoulder with them elves firing arrows.

Granny And it meant less chance of one hitting me, too. She'd been hit already. If I'd been hit too, neither of us'd get out.

Nanny But that's — that's a bit heartless, Esme.

Granny Heartless it may be, but headless it ain't. I've never claimed to be nice. Just sensible. Now, are you coming or are you going to stand there with your mouth open all day?

Nanny What're you going to do?

Granny Well, do you know how to cure her?

Nanny Me? No.

Granny Me neither. But I know someone who might know. And we can shove him in the dungeons for now. Lots of iron bars down there. That should keep him quiet.

Nanny How'd he get through?

Granny He was holding on to me. I don't know how it works. Just so long as his friends stay inside, that's all I'm bothered about.

Nanny Smell's worse than the bottom of a goat's bed. It's a bath for me when I get home.

Granny, Nanny and Diamanda exit

Black-out

Music plays : "Never Wed an Old Man"

SCENE 9

Lancre Castle

There is a long dining table, laid for dinner, and two chairs on stage

The main stage is lit. The music fades

Magrat and Verence are eating dinner at opposite ends of the table. Mr Spriggins, the butler, is serving them

Magrat Pardon?
Verence We need a ...
Magrat Sorry?
Verence What?
Magrat What?

After a pause Magrat gets up. Mr Spriggins moves Magrat's chair towards Verence with great difficulty. Magrat waits. The chair is placed nearer Verence and Magrat sits again

Verence We ought to have a Poet Laureate. Kingdoms have to have one. They write poems for special celebrations. I thought perhaps Mrs Ogg? I hear she's quite an amusing songstress.
Magrat I — er — I think she knows lots of rhymes for certain words. What exactly will she have to do?
Verence It says here the role of the Poet Laureate is to recite poems on state occasions.
Magrat Provided, and I want to be absolutely sure you understand me on this, provided she takes up her post after the wedding.
Verence Oh, dear? Really?
Magrat After the wedding.

There is a commotion, off

Shawn Ogg, Nanny and Granny enter, carrying Diamanda

Shawn Oooaaww, Mum! I'm supposed to go in first to say who it is!
Nanny We'll tell them who we are. Wotcha, your majesty.
Granny Blessings be upon this castle. Magrat, there's some doctorin' needs doing here. (*She lays Diamanda on the table*)
Magrat But I thought she was fighting you yesterday! What happened to her?
Granny She was shot by an elf ....
Magrat ⎫
Verence ⎬ (*together*) But ——
Granny Don't ask questions now, got no time. Shot by an elf. Them horrible arrows of theirs. They make the mind go wandering off all by itself. Now — can you do anything?
Magrat Oh, so suddenly I'm a witch again when you — —
Granny No time for that, either. I'm just askin'. All you have to do is say no. Then I'll take her away and won't bother you again.

Magrat I wasn't saying I wouldn't. (*She examines Diamanda*) Well, there's no fever. Slow pulse. Eyes unfocused. Shawn?
Shawn Yes, Miss Queen?
Magrat Run down to my cottage and bring back all the books you can find. On your way out, stop off in the kitchens and ask them to boil a lot of water.

Shawn exits

But look — elves ...
Granny I'll let you get on with it, then. Can I have a word with you, your majesty?

Granny and Verence move out of the hearing of Magrat and Nanny

During the following, Magrat and Nanny exit and return with water, bandages etc.

Shawn enters with books, mouldy bread and blankets, which he takes to Nanny and Magrat

Magrat and Nanny busy themselves with healing Diamanda

Verence What's happening, Mistress Weatherwax?
Granny Got something to show you.

Granny and Verence look off stage

Verence Good grief! That's an elf? But it's — just a long, thin human with a foxy face. More or less. I thought they were supposed to be beautiful?
Granny Oh, they are when they're conscious. They project this ... this ... When people look at them, they see beauty, they see something they want to please. They can look just like you want them to look. S'called glamour. You can tell when elves are around. People act funny. They stop thinking clear. Don't you know anything?
Verence I thought — elves were just stories — like the Tooth Fairy.
Granny Nothing funny about the Tooth Fairy. Very hardworking woman. I'll never know how she manages with the ladder and everything. No. Elves are real. Oh, drat. Listen; feudal system, right? King on top, then barons and whatnot, then everyone else ... Witches off to one side a bit. Feudal system. Understand?
Verence Yes.
Granny Right. That's how elves see things, yes? When they get into a world, everyone else is on the bottom. Slaves. Worse than slaves. Worse than animals even. They take what they want, and they want everything.

But worst of all — they read your mind. They hear what you think, and in self-defence you think what they want. Glamour. And it's barred windows at night, and food out for the fairies, and turning around three times before you talks about 'em and horseshoes over the door.

Verence I thought that sort of thing, was, you know, "folklore"?

Granny Of course it's folklore, you stupid man!

Verence I do happen to be king, you know.

Granny You stupid king, your majesty.

Verence Thank you.

Granny I mean it doesn't mean it's not true! Maybe it gets a little muddled over the years, folks forget details, they forget why they do things. The thing about elves is they got no ... Begins with M.

Verence Manners.

Granny Hah! Right, but no.

Verence Muscle? Mystery? Mucus?

Granny No. No. No. Means like — seein' the other person's point of view.

Verence Empathy?

Granny Right. None at all. Even a hunter, a good hunter can feel for the quarry. Elves aren't like that. They're cruel for fun, and they can't understand things like mercy. They laugh a lot, especially if they've caught a lonely human or a dwarf or a troll.

Verence But why don't I know all this?

Granny Glamour. Elves are beautiful. They've got style. If cats looked like frogs we'd realize what nasty, cruel little bastards they are. Style. That's what people remember.

Verence Magrat's never said anything about them.

Granny Magrat doesn't know too much about elves. They're not something that gets talked about a lot these days. It's not good to talk about them. It's better if everyone forgets them. They — come when they're called. It's enough for people to just want them to be here.

Verence I'm still learning about monarchy. I don't understand this stuff.

Granny Just go on reigning. I think we're safe. They can't get through. I've stopped the girls, so there'll be no more channelling. You keep this one firmly under lock and key, and don't tell Magrat. No sense in worrying her, is there? I think I've got it sorted ... What did I just say?

There is a sinister sound effect, as in Scene 5

Verence Uh. You said you thought you'd got it sorted.

Granny Yes. And I'm in the castle aren't I? Yes.

Verence Are you all right, Mistress Weatherwax?

Granny Fine, fine. Fine. In the castle. And the children are all right, too?

Verence Sorry? You don't look well ...

Granny Yes. The castle. I'm me, you're you. Just a bit of ... overtiredness there. Nothing to worry about. Nothing to worry about at all.

Granny and Verence move back to Nanny and Magrat

Nanny A mouldy bread poultice doesn't sound very magical to me.

Magrat Goodie Whemper used to swear by it. But I don't know what we can do about the coma. Elves don't shoot people. Elves are good.

Nanny They probably just fired at Esme and the girl in fun, like? Look, dear, you're going to be Queen. It's an important job. You look after the King now, and let me and Esme look after — other stuff.

Magrat Being Queen? It's all tapestry and walking around in unsuitable dresses! Um, Nanny? Would you like to be a bridesmaid?

Nanny Not really dear. Bit old for that sort of thing.

Granny How's the girl?

Magrat We took out the arrow and cleared up the wound. But she won't wake up. Best if she stays here.

Granny You sure? She needs keeping an eye on. I've got a spare bedroom. They've put their mark on her. You sure you know how to deal with it?

Magrat I do know it's a nasty wound.

Granny I ain't exactly thinking about the wound. She's been touched by them is what I mean.

Magrat I'm sure I know how to deal with a sick person. I'm not totally stupid, you know.

Granny She's not to be left alone.

Verence There'll be plenty of people around. The guests start arriving tomorrow.

Granny Being alone isn't the same as not having other people around.

Magrat This is a castle, Granny.

Granny Right. Well. We won't keep you, then. Come Gytha.

Nanny Have fun. Insofar as that's possible.

Granny and Nanny exit

Magrat What are they doing, those two?

Verence I don't know.

Magrat You're king, aren't you?

Verence But they're witches. I don't like to ask them questions.

Magrat What did Granny want to talk to you about?

Verence Oh ...You know — things ...

Magrat It wasn't about — sex, was it?

Verence No! Why?

Magrat Nanny was trying to give me motherly advice. It was all I could

do to keep a straight face. Er ... You did send off for that book, did you?
You know — the one with the woodcuts?

Verence Oh, yes. Yes, I did.

Magrat It ought to have arrived by now.

Verence Well, we only get a mail coach once a week. I expect it'll come
tomorrow. I'm fed up with running down there every week in case
Shawn gets there first.

Magrat You are king. You could tell him not to.

Verence Don't like to really. He's so keen.

Magrat Can you really get books about — that?

Verence You can get books about anything. Well, that's about it, then.
Busy day tomorrow, what with the guests coming and everything.

"As Time Goes By" from Casablanca plays

Magrat Yes. It's going to be a long day.

Verence So we'd better be off to bed, then, do you think?

Magrat I suppose so.

Verence Good-night, then.

Magrat Good-night.

Magrat and Verence kiss awkwardly, turn in opposite directions and exit

Black-out

SCENE 10

Lancre Bridge

The main stage and balcony are lit

A large troll stands on the balcony, waiting by the bridge

*The Bursar, Ridcully, Casanunda, Ponder and the Librarian enter on the
main stage level*

*Ridcully, followed by the Bursar, sets off up the stairs. During the following
Casanunda, Ponder and the Librarian follow them*

Bursar What's up?

Ridcully There's a troll on the bridge, but it's underneath a helmet so
it's probably official and will get into serious trouble if it eats people.
Nothing to worry about.

Troll Afternoon, your lordships. Customs inspection.

Bursar I don't think we have any. I mean we used to have a tradition of rolling boiled eggs downhill on Soul Cake Tuesday, but …

Troll I means do you have any beer, spirits, wines, liquors, hallucinogenic herbage or books of a lewd or licentious nature?

Ridcully No.

Troll Sure?

Ridcully Yes.

Troll Would you like some?

Bursar We haven't even got any billygoats. So we'll just trit trot along, shall we?

Ridcully He doesn't mean it. It's the dried frog talking.

Bursar You don't want to eat me. You want to eat my brother, he's much ——

Ridcully claps his hand over the Bursar's mouth

Mfmfph mfmfph …

Troll Well now, seems to me that … (*He spots Casanunda*) Oho, dwarf smuggling, eh?

Ridcully Don't be ridiculous man, there's no such thing ...

Troll Yeah? (*He looks at Casanunda*) Then what's that you've got there?

Casanunda I'm a giant.

Troll Giants are a lot bigger.

Casanunda I've been ill.

Troll (*pointing at the Librarian*) What's in that sack down there?

Ponder That's not a sack. That's the Librarian.

Librarian Ook ....

Troll What? A monkey?

Librarian (*angrily*) Oook?

The Librarian runs up the stairs, grabs the Troll and takes him off stage. There is a loud splash followed by a satisfied "Ook!"

Casanunda Do you think trolls can swim?

Ridcully (*leaning on the bridge*) No. They just sink and walk ashore. This really takes me back, you know. The old Lancre River. On this very bridge I asked ——

Ponder (*looking over the other side of the bridge*) He's got out of the river.

Casanunda That's a big club he's got.

Ridcully The actual bridge, if anyone's interested, is where my whole life took a diff …

Ponder Why don't we just go on? He's got a steep climb.

The Librarian enters

Casanunda Are you coming or not?

Ridcully I was actually having a quality moment of misty nostalgic remembrance. Not that any of you buggers noticed.

Ponder Well, you know what they say. You can't cross the same river twice, Archancellor.

Ridcully Why not? This is a bridge.

They exit

Black-out

SCENE 11

The Dancers

Three stones are visible at the back of the stage

The main stage is lit

The Rude Mechanicals — Jason, Obidiah, Weaver, Thatcher, Carter and Baker — enter carrying props, scripts, bundles and jugs of "scumble" — an alcoholic beverage similar to scrumpy — and singing "The Blackbird Song"

They all sit down and begin to drink scumble

Weaver You'd have thought the Blasted Oak would've been safe. Half a mile from the nearest path, and damn me if after five minutes you can't move for charcoal burners, hermits, trappers, dwarfs, bodgers and suspicious buggers with big coats on. I'm surprised there's room in the forest for the bloody trees. Where to now?

Obidiah Don't remember this one. Thought I knew all the paths round here.

Jason Let's go right.

Thatcher Nah, it's all briars and thorns that way.

Jason All right, then, left then.

Weaver It's all winding.

Carter What about the middle road?

Jason Not that way.

Weaver Ah, come on. What's wrong with it?

Jason Goes up to the Dancers, that path does. Me mam said no-one was to go up to the Dancers 'cos of them young women dancing round 'em in the nudd.

Thatcher Yeah, but they've been stopped from that. Old Granny Weath-erwax put her foot down and made 'em put their drawers on.

Carter And they ain't to go there any more, neither. So it'll be nice and quiet for rehearsing.

Jason Me mam said no-one was to go there.

Carter Yeah, but she probably meant — you know — with magical intent. Nothing magical about prancing about in wigs and stuff.

Baker Right. And it'll be really private.

Weaver And if any young women fancies sneaking back up there to dance around without their drawers on, we'll be sure to see 'em.

Pause

Thatcher I reckon we owes it to the community.

Jason We-ell, me mam said ——

Weaver Anyway your mum's a fine one to talk. My dad said that when he was young, your mum hardly ever had ——

Jason Oh, all right. Can't see it can do any harm. We're only actin'. It's ... It's make-believe. It's not as if it's anything real. But no-one's to do any dancing. Especially, and I want everyone to be absolutely definite about this, the Stick and Bucket Dance.

Carter Good-morrow, brothers, and wherehap do we whist this merry day?

Weaver You on some kind of medication or what?

Carter Just trying to enter into the spirit of the thing. That's how Rude Mechanicals talk.

Baker Who're Rude Mechanicals?

Carter They're the same as comic artisans, I think.

Jason I asked my mum what artisans are. They're us.

Baker And we're Rude Mechanicals as well?

Jason I reckon.

Baker Bum!

Carter Well, we certainly don't talk like these buggers in the writing. I never said "fol-de-rol" in my life. And I don't understand any of the jokes.

Jason You ain't supposed to understand the jokes, this is a play.

Baker Drawers!

Jason Oh, shut up.

Thatcher (*examining a script*) Don't work, does it?

Weaver S'not funny, that I do know. Can't see the king killing himself laughing at us playing a bunch of mechanical artisans not being very good at doin' a play.

Jason You're just no good at it.

Weaver We're s'posed to be no good at it.

Obidiah Yeah, but you're no good at acting like someone who's no good at acting. I don't know how, but you ain't. You can't expect all the fine lords and ladies to laugh at us being any good at being no good at acting.

Weaver I don't see what's funny about a bunch of rude artisans trying to do a play anyway.

Jason It says all the gentry in Ankh-Morpork laughed at it for weeks and weeks. It was on the Broad Way for three months.

Weaver They'd laugh at any damn thing down there. Anyway, they all think we'm simpletons up here. They all think we say "oo-aah" and sings daft folk songs and has three brain cells huddlin' together for warmth 'cos of drinking scumble all the time.

Baker Yeah. Pass that jug. Swish city bastards.

Carter They don't know what it's like to be up to the armpit in a cow's backside on a snowy night. Hah!

Weaver And there ain't one of 'em that ... What're you talking about? You ain't got a cow.

Carter No, but I know what's it's like.

Weaver They don't know what it's like to get one wellie sucked off in a farmyard full of gyppoe and that horrible moment where you waves your foot around knowin' that wherever you puts it down it's going to go through the crust.

Thatcher The point is. The point is. The point. The point is. Hah. All laughin' at decent rude artisans, eh? I mean. I mean. I mean. What's it all about? I mean. I mean. Play's all about some mechanical — rude buggers makin' a pig's ear out of doin' a play about a bunch of lords and ladies.

Elf 2 (*off*) It needs something else.

Weaver Right. Right.

Elf 2 (*off*) A mythic element.

Thatcher Right. My point. My point. Needs a plot they can go home whis'lin'. Exactly.

Elf 2 (*off*) So it should be done here, in the open air. Open to the sky and the hills.

Jason (*uncertainly*) Out here.

Weaver Good idea.

Jason Wasn't it your idea?

Weaver I thought you said it.

Thatcher Who cares who said it? S'a good idea. Seems — right.

Obidiah What was that about the miffic quality?

Weaver Something you've got to have. Very important, your miffics.

Jason Me mam said no-one was to go ...

Carter We shan't be doing any dancing or anything. It can't be wrong if everyone comes up here. I mean the king and everyone. Your mam, too. Hah, I'd like to see any girls with no drawers on get past her!

Weaver And the other one'll be there, too. Mistress Weatherwax.

Thatcher Cor, she frightens the life out of me, her. The way she looks right through you. (*He shouts loudly, in case Mistress Weatherwax can hear him*) I wouldn't say a word against her, mind you. A fine figure of a woman — (*quietly*) but they do say she creeps around the place o' nights, as a hare or a bat or something. (*Loudly*) Not that I believe a word of it.

Jason Reckon we ought to go home now, lads.

Baker S'nice night. Look at them stars a-twin'lin'.

Jason Turned a bit cold, though.

Carter Smells like snow.

Baker Oh, yeah. Snow at midsummer.

Jason Shut up! It's wrong. We shouldn't be up here. Can't you feel it?

Weaver Oh, sit down, man. It's fine. Can't feel nothing but the air. And there's still more scumble in the jug.

Baker You know, it does smell a bit like snow.

Jason Hey, lads. I've got 'nother jug coolin' in the water trough down in the forge, what d'you say? We could all go down there now. Lads? Lads?

All but Jason fall asleep. There is the sound of snoring

Oh, lads. (*He stands up and sways, and falls to the ground. He begins to snore*)

The Lights dim. A red wash of Light comes from the stone circle

Elves appear from behind the stones and draw their knives

The Elves look threateningly out towards the audience

The sinister sound effect is heard

Black-out

ACT II

The Dancers

The main stage is lit

Music plays

*The Rude Mechanicals are asleep on the ground as at the end of ACT I.
They slowly wake up and stagger about in hangover hell*

Jason (*kicking Carter*) Wake up, you ole bugger. We've been up here
all night!

Carter I'm going to get some stick from our Eva when I get home.

Thatcher You might not. Maybe when you gets home she'll have married someone else, eh?

Carter Maybe a hundred years have gone past!

Weaver Cor, I hope so. I had sevenpence invested in The Thrift Bank
down in Ohulan. I'll be a millionaire at the complicated interest. I'll
be as rich as Creosote.

Thatcher Who's Creosote?

Baker Some rich bugger. Foreign.

Carter Wasn't he the one, everything he touched turned into gold?

Obidiah Nah, that was someone else. Some king or other. That's what
happens in foreign parts. One minute you're all right, the next minute,
everything you touch turns into gold. He was plagued with it.

Carter How did he manage when he had to ...

Baker Let that be a lesson to you, young Carter. You stay here where folks
are sensible, not go gadding off abroad where you might suddenly be
holding a fortune in your hands and not have anything to spend it on.

Jason We've slept up here all night. That's dangerous, that is.

Carter You're right there, Mr Ogg. I think something went to the toilet
in my ear.

Jason I mean strange things can enter your head.

Carter That's what I meant too.

Jason Oh well, probably no harm done. Let's get on home to see what
century it is.

Black-out

Scene 2

Lancre Castle

The entire stage is lit

The Bursar, Ridcully, Casanunda, Ponder and the Librarian enter on to the balcony with the mail sack

Ridcully Can't you smell that? That's real fresh mountain air that is.
Ponder I've just trodden in something rural.
Ridcully Oh, my word. It all comes back to me ... What a summer that was. You know. I'd give anything to walk through those woods with her again... You'd just better taste the beer here! And there's stuff called scumble, they make it from apples ... You ought to try it, Mr Stibbons. It'd put hair on your chest and yours ...
Librarian Oook?
Ridcully Well, I — er — I should just drink anything you like, in your case. (*Referring to the mail sack*) What do we do with this?

Shawn Ogg enters on the main stage

(*Shouting down to Shawn*) What do we do with the mail?
Shawn I take the palace stuff, and we generally leave the sack hanging up on a nail outside the tavern so that everyone can help themselves.

Everyone on the balcony descends to the main stage

Ponder Isn't that dangerous?
Shawn Don't think so. It's a strong nail.
Ponder I meant, don't people steal letters?
Shawn Oh, they wouldn't do that. One of the witches'd go and stare at 'em if they did that.
Ridcully Yes, that's another thing they used to have round here. Witches! Let me tell you about the witches ...
Shawn Our mum's a witch.
Ridcully As fine a body of women as you could hope to meet. And not a bunch of interfering power-mad old crones at all, whatever anyone might say.
Shawn Are you here for the wedding?
Ridcully That's right. I'm the Archancellor of the Unseen University, this is Mr Stibbons, a wizard, this (*he looks round for Casanunda*) — where are you? Oh, there you are — this is Mr Casanunda.
Casanunda Count. I'm a count.

Ridcully Really? You never said. My word. And that's the Bursar and this is the Librarian. (*He mimes "Don't say monkey"*)
Shawn Pleased to meet you. How do you do?
Librarian Ook.
Ridcully You might be wondering why he looks like that ...
Shawn No, sir.
Ridcully No?
Shawn My mum says none of us can help how we're made.
Ridcully What a singular lady. Now that is what I call fresh air.
Shawn Yes, sir. That's what we call it too.

Verence runs on, but slows to a walk when he sees Shawn

It's the King! And me without my trumpet!
Verence Um ... Post been yet, Shawn?
Shawn Oh yes, sire! Got it right here. Don't you worry about it! I'll open it all up and have it on your desk right away, sire!
Verence Um ...
Shawn (*tearing open letters and parcels*) Something the matter sire?
Verence Um ... I think perhaps ...
Shawn Here's that book on etiquette you've been waiting for sire, and the pig stock book, and ... what's this one ... ?

Verence tries to grab this last book from Shawn but Shawn hangs on to it. In the struggle the wrapping falls off and the book falls open to the floor. They all look down

Wow!
Ridcully My word!
Verence Um.
Librarian Oook?
Shawn (*picking the book up*) Hey, look at this one! He's doing it with his feet! I didn't know you could do it with your feet!
Ridcully You all right, your majesty?
Verence Um ...
Shawn And, look, here's one where both chaps are doing it with sticks.
Verence What?
Shawn Wow! Thank you, sire. This is going to come in handy, I can tell you. I mean, I've picked up bits and pieces here and there, but ——
Verence (*snatching the book*) "Martial Arts?" Martial Arts. But I'm sure I wrote "Marit..."
Shawn Sire?
Verence Ah. Yes. Right. Uh. Well, yes. Of course. Yes. well, you see, a

well- trained army is — is essential to the security of the kingdom. That's right. Yes. Magrat and me, we thought … yes. It's for you, Shawn.

Shawn I'll start practising right away , sire!

The Bursar, Ridcully, Casanunda, Ponder, the Librarian and Shawn exit

Magrat and Millie enter on the balcony. Magrat is carrying a fan

Magrat I just saw a monkey walk across the square.

Millie The whole world's coming to Lancre!

Magrat This is stupid!

Millie What can you mean, ma'am?

Magrat All this? For me! I'm just Magrat Garlick! Kings ought to marry princesses and duchesses and people like that! People who are used to it! I don't want people shouting hooray just because I've gone by in a coach. All this — this — this stuff … it's not for me. It's for some idea. Didn't you ever get those cut-outs, those dolls, you know, when you were a girl — dolls you cut out, and there were cut-out clothes as well? And you could make her anything you wanted? That's me! I'm being turned into a queen whether I want to or not. That's what's happening to me!

Millie But you were the one who fell in love with the King, ma'am.

Magrat No. He wasn't a king then. No-one knew he was going to be king. He was just a sad, nice little man in a cap and bells, who everyone ignored.

Millie I expect it's nerves, ma'am. Everyone feels nervous on the day before their wedding. Shall I … Shall I see if I can make you some herbal ——

Magrat I'm not nervous! And I can do my own herbal tea if I happen to want any!

Millie Cook's very particular who goes into the herb garden, ma'am.

Magrat I've seen that herb garden! It's all leggy sage and yellowy parsley! If you can't stuff it up a chicken's bum, she doesn't think it's a herb! Anyway — who's queen in this vicinity?

Millie I thought you didn't want to be, ma'am?

Magrat throws her fan at Millie who dodges and escapes

Millie exits

Shawn Ogg brings Diamanda on and lays her down on the floor. He exits and returns with several heavy iron objects, some wrapped in cloth, which he lays in a circle around Diamanda

Magrat descends the ladder to the stage and examines Diamanda

Magrat What are all these things?

Shawn The King said — well, Granny said ...

Magrat Granny Weatherwax does not happen to rule the kingdom. And anyway she is not here. One is here, however, and if you don't tell one what's going on I'll see to it that you do all the dirty jobs around the palace.

Shawn But I do all the dirty jobs anyway.

Magrat I shall see to it that there are dirtier ones. They're all around her. Why?

Shawn Our mum said I was to see to it that there was iron round her. So me and Millie got some bars from down the smithy and wrapped 'em up like this and Millie packed 'em round her.

Magrat Why?

Shawn To keep away the — Lords and Ladies, ma'am.

Magrat What? That's just superstition! Anyway, everyone knows elves were good, whatever Granny Weatherwax says. No old wives' tales here, thank you very much. Well. Go away.

Shawn Yes, Miss Queen.

Magrat Shawn?

Shawn Yes, ma'am?

Magrat Has the King gone down to the Great Hall yet?

Shawn I think he's still dressing, Miss Queen. He hasn't rung for me to do the trumpet, I know that.

Black-out

SCENE 3

Lancre Castle

The main stage is lit

Verence, the Bursar, Ridcully, Casanunda, Ponder, the Librarian and the guests are on the main stage, being served food and drink by Mr Spriggins and others

Nanny and Granny enter

Granny and Ridcully start the scene at some distance from each other and cannot see each other through the crowd

Nanny All the hort mond are here. Even some wizards from Ankh-Morpork, our Shawn said.

Granny There's some gentry we don't want to see here. I won't be happy until all this is over.

Nanny Can't see Magrat around. There's Verence talking to some other
kings, but can't see our Magrat at all. Our Shawn said Millie Chillum
said she was just a bag of nerves this morning.

Granny Don't drink too much. We've got to keep alert, Gytha. Remember
what I said. Don't let yourself get distracted.

Casanunda That's never the delectable Mrs Ogg, is it? Down here.

Nanny Oh, blast.

Casanunda It's me, Casanunda. You remember? We danced the night
away in Genua?

Nanny No, we didn't.

Casanunda Well, we could have done. Our stars are entwined. We're
fated for one another. I wants your body, Mrs Ogg.

Nanny I'm still using it. It'd never work. We're basically incompatible.
I'm old enough to be your mother.

Casanunda You can't be. My mother's nearly three hundred, and she's
got a better beard than you.

Nanny La, sir you do know how to turn a simple country girl's head
and no mistake!

Nanny hits Casanunda playfully and he falls to the floor

Casanunda (*picking himself up*) I like a girl with spirit. How about you
and me having a little tête-à-tête when this is over?

Nanny You're on.

Casanunda I thought we could have a little private dinner, just you and me.
In one of the taverns. Dodge your chaperone and meet me at six o'clock.

Nanny She's not my ... Yes, all right.

Casanunda And now I shall circulate, so that people don't talk and ruin
your reputation.

Granny You haven't got the morals of a cat, Gytha Ogg.

Nanny Now, Esme, you know that's not true.

Granny All right. You have got the morals of a cat. We must stay on
our guard, Gytha.

Nanny Yes, yes.

Granny Can't let other considerations turn our heads.

Nanny No, no.

Granny You're not listening to a word I say, are you?

Nanny What?

Granny You could at least find out why Magrat isn't down here.

Nanny All right. (*She turns as if to wander away*)

Ridcully (*spotting Granny from across the stage*) Esme?

Granny Mustrum?

Nanny Esme, I saw Millie Chillum and she said ——

Granny elbows Nanny in the ribs

Ah, I'll just, I'll just ... I'll just go away then. (*She moves away*)
Bursar I say, Archancellor, these quails' eggs are amazingly goo —
Ridcully Drop dead. Mr Stibbons, fish out the frog pills and keep knives
away from him, please.

*During the following, Granny and Ridcully approach each other through
the crowd, which parts for them*

Granny Well, well.
Ridcully This must be some enchanted evening.
Granny Yes. That's what I'm afraid of.
Ridcully You haven't changed a bit, Esme.
Granny Nor have you then. You're still a rotten liar, Mustrum Ridcully.
Ridcully Small world.
Granny Yes, indeed.
Ridcully You're you and I'm me. Amazing. And it's here and now.
Granny Yes, but then was then.
Ridcully I sent you a lot of letters.
Granny Never got 'em.
Ridcully That's odd. And there was me putting all those destination spells
on them too. How much do you weigh, Esme? Not a spare ounce on
you, I'll be bound.
Granny What do you want to know for?
Ridcully Indulge an old man.
Granny Nine stones, then.
Ridcully Hmmm — should be about right ... Three miles hubwards ...
You'll feel a slight lurch to the left, nothing to worry about. Let me
take you away from all this.

*Ridcully grabs Granny's arm and snaps his fingers. There is a "magical"
sound effect and a pyrotechnic explosion. Black-out*

Granny and Ridcully exit

*Some of the guests take up compromising positions. Casanunda and a
guest take up a sexual position, the guest's consort picks the pocket of a
neighbour, etc.*

Magrat, as yet not visible, stands behind the door

The Lights come up on Nanny and Verence, who are standing by the door

Nanny What's happening?
Verence I know she's in there. Millie heard her shout "Go away" and I think she threw something at the door.
Nanny Wedding nerves. Bound to happen.

Shawn Ogg enters with a sign saying "Coaches to the Entertainment". The guests file off in twos and threes during the following, including Casanunda and his latest conquest

Verence But we're all going to attend the Entertainment. She really ought to attend the Entertainment.
Nanny Well, I dunno. Seeing our Jason and the rest of them prancing about in straw wigs ... I mean, they mean well but it's not something a young — a fairly young — girl has to see on the night before her nuptials. You asked her to unlock the door?
Verence I did better than that. I instructed her to. That was right, wasn't it? If even Magrat won't obey me, I'm a poor lookout as king.
Nanny Ah ... You've not entirely spent a lot of time in female company, have you? In a generalized sort of a way? Tell you what, you go with the other nobs. I'll see to Magrat, don't you worry. I been a bride three times, and that's only the official score.
Verence Yes, but she should ...
Nanny I think if we go easy on the "shoulds" we might all make it to the wedding. Now off you go.
Verence Someone ought to stay here. Shawn will be on guard but ——
Nanny No-one's going to invade, are they? Let me sort this out ... Go on!

Verence, the remaining guests and Shawn exit

Magrat?
Magrat (*from behind the door*) Go away!
Nanny I know how it is. I was a bit worried on the night before my wedding.
Magrat I am not worried! I am angry!
Nanny Why?
Magrat You know!
Nanny You've got me there.
Magrat And he knew. I know he knew, and I know who told him. It was all arranged. You must have all been laughing!
Nanny Nope. Still all at sea this end.
Magrat Well, I'm not saying any more.
Nanny Everyone's gone to the Entertainment — and later they'll be back ... Then there will be carousing and jugglers and fellas that put weasels down their trousers — and then it'll be tomorrow, and then what're you

going to do? You can always go back to your cottage. No-one's moved in. Or you can stop along with me if you like. But you'll have to decide, d'you see, because you can't stay locked in there ... So I'll be off then, shall I? Not doing much good here, I can see that. Sure you don't want to talk? Tell you what, I'll come back early tomorrow, help you get ready, that sort of thing. How about it? So that's all sorted then. Cheerio.

Casanunda enters and approaches Nanny

Casanunda 'Allo, o moon of my delight.
Nanny You do sneak up on people, Casanunda.
Casanunda I've arranged for us to have dinner at the Goat and Bush.
Nanny Ooo, that's a horrible expensive place. Never eaten there.
Casanunda They've got special provisions in, what with the wedding and all the gentry here, I've made special arrangements.

Black-out

SCENE 4

Lancre Bridge

The balcony is lit

Granny and Ridcully are on stage

Granny Take me back this instant. You've got no right to do that!
Ridcully Dear me, I seem to have run out of power. Can't understand it, very embarrassing, fingers gone all limp. Of course, we could walk. It's a lovely evening. You always did get lovely evenings here. Do you remember?
Granny I have a — very good memory, thank you.
Ridcully Do you ever wonder what life would have been like if you'd said yes?
Granny No.
Ridcully I suppose we'd have settled down, had children, grandchildren, that sort of thing ...
Granny What about the fire? Swept through our house just after we were married. Killed us both.
Ridcully What fire? I don't know anything about any fire.
Granny Of course not! It didn't happen. But the point is, it might have happened. You can't say, "if this didn't happen then that would have happened" because you don't know everything that might have happened. You'll never know. You've gone past. So there's no use thinking about it. So I don't.

Ridcully The Trousers of Time.

Granny What?

Ridcully That's the sort of thing they go on about in the High Energy Magic building. And they call themselves wizards! Trousers of Time. One of you goes down one leg, one of you goes down the other. And there's all these continuinuinuum's all over the place. When I was a lad there was just one decent universe and this was it. Now it turns out there's millions of the damn things. And they all run around saying "Marvellous, marvellous, hooray, here comes another quantum." You should hear young Stibbons talk. Went on about me not inviting me to my own wedding. Me! Kept going on about everything happening at the same time. He says that we did get married, see. He says all the things that might have been have to be. So there's thousands of me out there who never became a wizard, just like there's thousands of you who, oh, answered letters.

Granny Stupid, stupid, stupid.

Ridcully I beg your pardon? I was only ——

Granny Not you. I wasn't talking to you. Stupid! I've been stupid. But I ain't been daft! Hah! And I thought it was my memory going! And it was, too. It was going and fetching.

Ridcully What?

Granny I was getting scared! Me! And not thinking clear! Except I was thinking clear. Never mind! Well, I won't say this hasn't been — nice. But I've got to get back. Do the thing with the fingers again. And hurry.

Ridcully Can't. I wasn't joking when I said I couldn't do it again. It takes a lot out of you, transmigration. What's the hurry?

Granny Got important things to do. Been letting everyone down. I'm too busy for this. Personal ain't the same as important. Make yourself useful Mr Wizard. It's circle time.

They exit

Music plays: "No Sir No"

Black-out

SCENE 5

The Entertainment

The balcony is lit

Ponder, the Bursar, the Librarian and the guests are on the balcony, staring out into the auditorium, watching the "Entertainment". The Librarian holds a bag of peanuts

During the following, Shawn Ogg enters on to the main stage (as yet unlit) and takes up a position as a guard

Librarian (*offering peanuts to Ponder*) Oook?

Ponder No, thank you. They give me wind.

Librarian (*offering nuts to the Bursar*) Oook?

Bursar I like to listen to a man who likes to talk! Whoops! Sawdust and treacle! Put that in your herring and smoke it!

Ponder (*to the Librarian*) I don't think he wants one. It's started.

Librarian Oook?

Ponder Quiet! They're getting the hang of it ... What'd she say?

Librarian Ooook!

Ponder How'd she do that? That's good make-up, that ... (*His eyes become glazed*)

The Bursar and the other guests — with the exception of the Librarian — glaze over as well. The Librarian waves a hand up and down in front of the Bursar's face

Elvish music is heard

Librarian Oook? Oook?

The Lights come up on the main stage

Shawn Ogg is on guard. He hears the strange music and is alarmed

Shawn Stop! Or ... or ... or ... stop! I warn you! I'm learning the Path of the Happy Lotus!

Diamanda and Elf 1 enter

Aren't you Miss Tockley?

Diamanda You're wearing chain-mail, Shawn.

Shawn What, miss?

Diamanda That's terrible. You must take it off, Shawn. How can you hear with all that stuff around your ears?

Shawn I can hear fine, miss.

Diamanda But you can't hear truly. The iron makes you deaf.

Diamanda and the Elf advance on Shawn. He runs

Shawn exits, followed by Diamanda and the Elf

Magrat enters wearing her wedding dress and carrying a bag. She hears the music, drops the bag and begins to sway

Shawn runs on and grabs Magrat, dragging her towards the wall

Shawn Are you all right, Miss Queen?

Magrat What's happening?

Shawn Dunno, Miss Queen. But I think we've got elves. And they've got Miss Tockley. Um. You know you took the iron away ...

Magrat What are you talking about, Shawn?

Shawn That one down in the dungeons started singing, and they'd put their mark on her, so she's doing what they want ... And Mum said they don't kill you, if they can help it. You're much more fun if you're not dead. I had to run away! She was trying to get my hood off! I had to leave her, miss! You've got to hold on to something iron, miss. They hate iron!

Magrat You're gabbling, Shawn!

Shawn They're out there, miss! I heard the drawbridge go down! They're out there and we're in here and they don't kill you, they keep you alive ...

Magrat Stand to attention, soldier! Look, everyone knows there really aren't any elves any mo ... Everyone but Magrat Garlick knows different, yes? (*She shakes Shawn*)

Shawn Me mum and Mistress Weatherwax said you wasn't to know! They said it was witches' business!

Magrat And where are they now, when they've got some witch business to mind? I don't see them, do you? There's just me, Shawn Ogg. And where's everyone now?

Shawn All gone to the Entertainment — but they ought to've been back by now. Why've you got your wedding dress on?

Magrat Never you mind.

Shawn It's unlucky for the groom to see the bride in her dress before the wedding.

Magrat It will be for him, if I see him first.

Shawn I'm feared about what's happened to everyone. Our Jason said they'd be back in an hour or so, and that was hours ago.

Magrat But there's almost a hundred guests and everyone from the town, practically. Elves couldn't do anything to them.

Shawn They wouldn't have to, miss. I can sneak around the kitchens and out by the little gate by the hubward tower with military precision.

Magrat What for?

Shawn To get help, miss.

Magrat But you don't know if there's any help to get.

Shawn Can you think of anything else, miss?

Magrat It's very — brave of you, Shawn.

Shawn You stay here and you'll be right as rain. Tell you what … How about if I lock the door and take the key with me? Then even if they sing at you they can't get you to open the door. Wish we had another suit of mail. But it's all in the armoury.

Magrat I'll be fine. Off you go, then.

Shawn exits

Magrat sits down and listens

There is silence, then a scream, off. There is the sound of someone scrabbling at the lock of the door

Elf 1 Will you not step outside, lady?

Elf 2 Will you not come dance with us, pretty lady?

Magrat climbs the ladder and runs across the balcony

There is the sound of a door opening

> *Three Elves burst on to the stage at the lower level. They look around and point up to the balcony where Magrat is running. They laugh and follow*

Black-out. A portrait of Queen Ynci, a former warrior queen of Lancre, dressed in female armour and a horned helmet, is placed on the lower stage

The Lights come up

> *Magrat appears on stage, breathless. She sees the portrait of Queen Ynci, then hearing the Elves laugh she runs off though the door*

Black-out

SCENE 6

The woods

The main stage and balcony are lit

Five Elves watch from the balcony. Some carry bows and arrows

Granny and Ridcully enter on to the main stage

Granny I keep tellin' you, I ain't lost. I'm — directionally challenged.

Ridcully Well, well. There's a familiar tree.

Granny Shut up.

Ridcully I thought someone said we just had to walk up the hill.
Granny Shut up.
Ridcully I remember once when we were in these woods you let me ——
Granny Shut up. We're being mazed. Someone's playing tricks on us. She's doing it. It's an elvish trick. Leading travellers astray. She's mucking up my head. Making us go where she wants. Making us go round in circles. Doing it to me.
Ridcully Maybe you've got your mind on other things.
Granny Course I've got my mind on other things, with you falling over all the time and gabbling a lot of nonsense. If Mr Cleverdick Wizard hadn't wanted to dredge up things that never existed in the first place, I wouldn't be here, I'd be in the centre of things, knowing what's going on.
Ridcully You looked pretty surprised when you saw me. Your face went white.
Granny Anyone'd go white, seeing a full-grown man standing there looking like a sheep about to choke.
Ridcully You really don't let up, do you? Amazing. You don't give an inch ... (*He notices the Elves*) You know either autumn comes really early in these parts, or someone's in the tree above us.
Granny I know. There's at least five of 'em and they're right above us. How's those magic fingers of yours?
Ridcully I could probably manage a fireball.
Granny Wouldn't work. Can you carry us out of here?
Ridcully Not both of us.
Granny Just you?
Ridcully Probably, but I'm not going to leave you.
Granny It's true, you know. All men are swains. Push off, you soft old bugger. They're not intending to kill me. At least, not yet. But they don't hardly know nothing about wizards and they'll chop you down without thinking.
Ridcully Now who's being soft?
Granny I don't want to see you dead when you could be doing something useful.
Ridcully I'd never forgive myself if I went.
Granny And I'd never forgive you if you stayed, and I'm a lot more unforgiving than you are. When it's all over, try to find Gytha Ogg. Tell her to look in my old box. She'll know what's in there. And if you don't go now ——

The Elves fire arrows at Granny and Ridcully

Ridcully The buggers are firing at me! If I had my crossbow ——
Granny I should go and get it, then.

Ridcully Right! I'll be back instantly.

There is a flash of light, then a Black-out

Ridcully exits

The Lights come back on

Granny That's him out of the way, then. All right here I am. I ain't running. Come and get me. Here I am. All of me.

Black-out

SCENE 7

Lancre Castle. Outside the armoury door

The main stage is lit

The portrait of Queen Ynci is on stage

Four Elves and Shawn Ogg are on stage. Magrat is behind the door

Elf 1 Lady? If lady wants to play, we will fetch her friends.
Elf 2 Come dance at the wedding, lady.
Elf 3 Lady? We will bring your friends to sing to you.
Elf 1 We wish the lady to come out. You must say to her, if she does not come out, we will play with you some more.
Shawn What will you do to me if she does come out?
Elf 2 Oh, we shall still play with you. That's what makes it so much fun. But she must hope, must she not? Talk to her now.
Shawn (*moving to the door*) Um. Miss Queen? It's me, Shawn.
Magrat (*from behind the door*) I know.
Shawn I'm out here. Um. I think they've hurt Miss Tockley. They say they'll hurt me some more if you don't come out. But you don't have to come out because they daren't come in there because of all the iron. So I shouldn't listen to them if I was you ... Miss Magrat?
Elf 4 Ask her if there is any food and water in there.
Shawn Miss, they say ——

Elf 3 pushes Shawn aside and puts his ear to the keyhole, then his eye. There is a click of a crossbow. Elf 3 falls to the floor, a crossbow bolt sticking out of its eye

Wow.

*The door swings open, revealing Magrat, holding the crossbow. Magrat
is also armed with a knife, as yet unseen*

Elf 2 (*laughing*) So much for him. How stupid … Lady? Will you listen
to your warrior?

Elf 2 twists Shawn's arm

Magrat All right. I'm going to come out. You must promise not to hurt me.
Elf 2 Oh, indeed I do, lady.
Magrat And you'll let Shawn go.
Elf 2 Yes. (*But he doesn't*)
Magrat (*placing the crossbow on the floor*) Remember you promised
not to hurt me.
Elf 2 Lady?
Magrat Yes?
Elf 2 I lied.

*Elf 1 and Elf 4 close in on Magrat from behind. Elf 4 raises a knife which he
plunges towards Magrat's back. It hits but has no effect. Magrat draws her
knife and stabs Elf 4, then kicks Elf 1 to the floor, where he lies, writhing*

Shawn, which one hurt you?
Shawn All of them. (*He indicates Elf 2*) But this one stabbed Diamanda.
Magrat Stop it. (*She raises the crossbow*)
Elf 2 I will not beg for mercy
Magrat Good.

Magrat shoots Elf 2. She then steps into the armoury and produces an axe

Elf 1 stops writhing on the floor and stares at Magrat

Now, I'm not going to lie to you about your chances, because you
haven't got any. I'm going to ask you some questions. But first of all,
I'm going to get your attention. (*She raises the axe and brings it down
to the* L *of the elf's head*)
Shawn Miss? Mum says they don't feel pain.
Magrat No? But they can certainly be put to inconvenience. Of course, there's
armour. We could put this one in a suit of armour. How about it?
Elf 1 No!

Magrat Why not? Better than axes, yes?
Elf 1 No! It is like being buried in the earth. No eyes, no ears, no mouth.
Magrat Chain mail, then.
Elf 1 No!
Magrat Where is the King? Where is everyone?
Elf 1 I will not say.
Magrat All right. (*She goes into the armoury and returns dragging a suit of chain mail*)

Elf 1 trys to crawl away

Shawn You won't get it on. You'll never get it over its arms.

Magrat picks up the axe

Oh, no. Miss!
Elf 2 You will never get him back. She has him.
Magrat We shall see. All right Shawn. What shall we do with it?

They lock the elf in the armoury

Now let's have a look at that arm of yours. (*She swings the axe during the following*)
Shawn I'm all right but they stabbed Diamanda in the kitchen. You killed them.
Magrat Did I do it wrong?
Shawn Um. No. No ... You did it quite well really.
Magrat Are there any more around?
Shawn I — don't think so. Uh. Miss Queen?
Magrat Yes, Shawn?
Shawn Could you put the axe down, please? I'd feel a lot better if you put the axe down. The axe, Miss Queen. You keep swinging it about. It could go off at any second.
Magrat What axe?
Shawn The one you're holding.
Magrat Oh, this axe. (*She lowers the axe*)Did they kill Diamanda?
Shawn I don't know. And I don't know why. I mean, she was helping them.
Magrat Yes. D'you know the funny thing about Lancre? We never throw anything away. And you know another thing? (*She points to the Queen Ynci portrait*) They couldn't have painted her from life, of course. But the armour ... hah! All they had to do was look. And you know what?
Shawn What, miss?
Magrat No-one told me about her. You'd think it's all tapestry and walking around in long dresses.

Shawn What, miss?

Magrat All this! (*She waves the axe*)

Shawn (*dropping to the floor*) Miss! Please put the axe down!

Magrat Oh. Sorry. (*She takes off her dress, revealing armour identical to Queen Ynci's underneath*) Use this to make bandages for Diamanda. Fairly good fit. Not that a few tucks and a rivet here and there wouldn't help. Don't you think it looks good?

Shawn Oh, yes. Sheet iron is really you.

Magrat You really think so?

Shawn Oh, yes. You've got the figure for it.

Magrat OK. I'll fetch a couple of crossbows and load them for you. And you keep the door shut and let no-one in, d'you hear? And if I don't come back — try and go somewhere where there's people. Get up to the dwarfs at Copperhead. Or the trolls.

Shawn What are you going to do?

Magrat I'm going to see what's happened to everyone.

Shawn But there's probably more of those things out there! Can you fight?

Magrat Don't know. Never tried.

Shawn But if we wait here, someone's bound to come.

Magrat Yes. I'm afraid they will.

Shawn What I mean is, you don't have to do this.

Magrat Yes I do. I'm getting married tomorrow. One way or the other.

Shawn But miss, if you don't come back ——

Magrat I'll be back.

Magrat exits

The music from "Terminator" plays

Shawn Good luck!

Black-out

Scene 8

The Dancers

Only some of the stones are visible; some of these have been knocked over

The main stage is lit

Jason, Obidiah, Thatcher, Carter and Baker are on stage. Carter carries a sack which contains Morris Men's equipment: bells, sticks, buckets and an accordion

Thatcher Jason?

Jason Is that you, Weaver?

Thatcher No, it's me — Thatcher.

Jason Where's everyone else?

Thatcher Baker found Obidiah just now. Have you seen Weaver?

Jason No, but I saw Bestiality Carter.

Carter There's going to be hell to pay in the morning! When she finds us we're done for!

Jason We'll be all right if we can find some iron.

Carter Iron doesn't have any effect on her! She'll tan our hides for us!

Jason Who?

Carter Mistress Weatherwax!

Thatcher Don't be so daft! You saw them things! What're you worrying about that old baggage for?

Carter She'll tan our hides for us, right enough! 'Twas all our fault, she'll say!

Baker I just hopes she gets the chance.

Obidiah What happened when we was doing the Ent …

Jason I ain't asking that question right now. The question I'm asking right now is, how do we get home tonight?

Carter She'll be waiting for us!

Jason What've you got there?

Carter It's the props sack. You said as how it was my job to look after the props sack.

Baker You dragged that all the way down here?

Carter I ain't about to get into more trouble 'cos of losing the props sack!

Jason If we gets home I'm going to talk to our mam about getting you some of these new dried frog pills … There's our bells in here and the sticks. And who told you to pack the accordion?

Carter I thought we might want to do the Stick and ——

Jason No-one's ever to do the Stick and ——

The laughter of Elves is heard off

Carter They're out there!

Obidiah And we ain't got any weapons.

Jason Shut up and put your bells on. Carter?

Carter They're waiting for us!

Jason I'll say this just once. After tonight no-one's ever to talk about the Stick and Bucket dance ever again. All right?

They put on their bells, pick up their sticks and ready themselves. Carter plays the accordion. The dance commences and continues throughout the following

One, two ... One, two, three — four. Dance lads! One, two, forward, one back, spin ... Two, back, jump.

Carter They're watching us! I can see 'em.

The Elves enter and begin to advance

Jason One ... Two ... They won't do nothing 'til the music stops! Back, two, spin ... They loves music! Forward, hop, turn ... One and six, beetle crushers! Hop, back, spin.

Obidiah They're coming out of the bracken!

Jason I see 'em ... Two, three, forward, turn ... Carter — back, spin ... You do a double — two, back — "Wandering Angus" down the middle ...

Carter I'm losing it, Jason!

Jason Play! Two, three, spin ...

Baker They're all around us!

Jason Dance!

Thatcher They're watching us! They're closing in!

Jason Remember when — three, turn — we won the cup against Ohulan Casuals? Spin —

Thatcher Jason, you don't mean ...

Jason Back, two — do it —

Baker Carter's getting — one, two — out of wind —

Carter The accordion's melting, Jason.

Jason One, two, forward —"Bean setting"!

Obidiah Jason!

Jason One, two ... Carter into the middle ... one, two, spin.

Obidiah Jason!

During the following, on each "Kill" the dancers strike the Elves, knocking them down

Jason One, two — spin — ready ... One, two — back — back ... One, two — turn — KILL — and back, one, two — turn — KILL ...

They dance off the stage

Black-out

SCENE 9

The Long Man; a burial mound

There are two standing stones at the bottom of the ladder. There is a smaller standing stone on the balcony; it features a symbol of a man painted in white, very much like the Cerne Abbas giant

The main stage and balcony are lit

Nanny and Casanunda appear on the balcony

Casanunda We were just getting to know one another properly and fifty
elves burst into the place! Damn! This kind of thing happens to me
all the time ... They aren't following us any more. We've frightened
them off, yes?

Nanny Not us. They're nervy of going close to the Long Man. It's not
their turf. Huh, look at the state of this path. When I was a girl, you
wouldn't find a blade of grass growing on the path. Very popular place
on a summer night, the Long Man was.

Casanunda It's just an old burial mound.

Nanny Three old burial mounds.

Casanunda Yes, I see them. Two round ones and a long one. Well?

Nanny The first time I saw 'em from the air, I nearly fell off the bloody
broomstick for laughin'.

Casanunda Blimey, I thought the people who built burial mounds and
earthworks were serious druids and people like that, not ... not people
who drew on privy walls with two hundred thousand tons of earth, in
a manner of speaking.

Nanny Doesn't sound like you to be shocked by that sort of thing.

Casanunda Well, there's such a thing as style. There's such a thing as
subtlety. You don't just shout "I've got a great big tonker!"

Nanny Esme doesn't ever come up here. She says it's bad enough about
folksongs and maypoles and suchlike, without the whole scenery getting suggestive. Course this was never intended as a woman's place.
My great-gran said in the real old days the men used to come up for
strange rites what no women ever saw.

Casanunda Except your great-grandmother, who hid in the bushes.

Nanny How did you know that?

Casanunda Let's just say I'm developing a bit of an insight into Ogg
womanhood, Mrs Ogg.

Casanunda Anyone ever worked out what that says?

Nanny It's a variant of Oggham. Basically it means, "I've got a great
big tonker."

Casanunda What is down there?

Nanny Well, it leads into Lancre Caves. They run everywhere. But mainly
they lead to the world of the elves.

Casanunda I thought the Dancers led to the world of the elves?

Nanny This is the other world of the elves.

Casanunda I thought they only had one.

Nanny They don't talk about this one.

Casanunda And you want to go in to it? You want to find elves?
Nanny Yes.

They climb down the ladder

They got put up at the same time as the Dancers. Might as well leave
our crowbar here and take your boots off if they've got nails in 'em.
Casanunda These boots were stitched by the finest shoemaker in Ankh-
Morpork and one day I shall pay him.

*Nanny and Casanunda move through the stones and stand facing the
audience, as if the Long Man is visible there*

Long Man (*offstage voice*) Ah. Mrs Ogg.
Nanny Y'lordship.
Long Man (*off*) I suppose it is too much to expect you to kneel.
Nanny Yes indeed, y'honour.
Long Man (*off*) You know, Mrs Ogg, you have a way of showing respect
to your god that would make the average atheist green with envy.
Nanny Thank you, y'grace.
Long Man (*off*) No-one even dances for me now. Is that too much to
ask? You witches don't believe in me any more.
Nanny Right again, your hornishness.
Long Man (*off*) Ah, little Mrs Ogg — and how, having got in here, do
you possibly think you are going to get out?
Nanny Because I have iron.
Long Man (*off*) Of course you have not, little Mrs Ogg. No iron can
enter this realm.
Nanny I have the iron that goes everywhere. (*She produces a horseshoe
from her knicker leg*)
Long Man (*off*) Take it away!
Nanny I'll take it away when I go. Now you listen to me. She's making
trouble again. You've got to put a stop to it. Fair's fair. We're not hav-
ing all the Old Trouble again.
Long Man (*off*) Why should I do that?
Nanny You want her to be powerful, then? You can't ever rule again,
back in the world. There's too much music. There's too much iron.
Long Man (*off*) Iron rusts.
Nanny Not the iron in the head.
Long Man (*off*) Nevertheless — even that ... one day.
Nanny One day. Yes, I'll drink to that. Who knows? One day. Everyone
needs "one day". But it ain't today. D'you see? So you come on out
and balance things up. Otherwise, this is what I'll do. I'll get 'em to

dig into the Long Man with iron shovels, y'see, and they'll say, why it's just an old earthworks, and pensioned off wizards and priests with nothin' better to do will pick over the heaps and write dull old books about burial traditions and suchlike, and that'll be another iron nail in your coffin. And I'd be a little bit sorry about that, 'cos you know I've always had a soft spot for you. But I've got kiddies y'see, and they don't hide under the stairs because they're frit, and they don't put milk out for the elves, and they don't hurry home because of the night, and before we go back to them dark old ways, I'll see you nailed.

Pause

Long Man (*off*) I — will decide.
Nanny Very good. You decide. And I'll be getting along.
Long Man (*off*) What are you staring at?
Nanny Go on, answer the nice gentleman.
Casanunda Blimey, you don't half look like your picture.

Black-out

Music plays

Scene 10

Lancre Square

The main stage is lit. The music fades

Weaver is on stage

Magrat enters with a crossbow and an axe. She is wearing armour and a "Queen Ynci" helmet

Magrat You're Carter the baker, aren't you?
Weaver I'm Weaver the thatcher.

Weaver moves to run away; Magrat blocks his path

Magrat You know who I am?
Weaver Miss Garlick? Are you alone, miss?
Magrat Yes. What's going on?
Weaver Er … Didn't recognize you in your flying hat, miss.
Magrat I thought you were doing the Entertainment? What's happened? Where is everyone? Where is my going-to-be-husband?

Weaver Er ...

Magrat grabs Weaver

Magrat If you say "Er" one more time I'll chop your ears off.
Weaver Er — aargh — I mean, miss ... It's the Lords and Ladies, miss!
Magrat Where did it happen?
Weaver Up at the Dancers, miss. You know. Them old stones.
Magrat Oh, yes. Don't tell Magrat. Magrat's not to know about this sort of thing. The Dancers? Right.
Weaver Where're you going, miss?
Magrat Where d'you think?
Weaver But, miss, you can't take iron ——
Magrat Go home.

Weaver exits. As he goes:

Three Elves — Lankin, Elf 1 and Elf 2, with bows and arrows — enter and step in front of Magrat

Lankin Good-evening, girl. My name is Lord Lankin, and you will curtsy when you talk to me.
Magrat I happen to be practically the queen.
Lankin There is only one queen in Lancre. And you are, most definitely, not her.
Magrat Where is she, then?

Elf 1 and 2 raise their bows

Lankin You are looking for the Queen? Then we will take you to her. And, lady, should you be inclined to make use of that nasty iron bow there are more archers hidden in the trees.

There are noises of crashes and thumps off stage

Magrat Get out of my way.
Elf 1 I think you have a very wrong idea.
Lankin We felt you coming all the way up the track. The brave girl off to rescue her lover! Oh, the romance! Take her.

The Librarian and Ponder enter behind Elf 1 and 2

The Librarian bangs the elves' heads together. He then knocks Lankin out

Librarian Oook?
Ponder Put the axe down please, miss!
Magrat Who are you?
Ponder Um, I'm Ponder Stibbons, a wizard. And he's a wizard too.
Magrat He's got no clothes on!
Ponder I could get him to have a bath if you like. He always puts on an
  old green dressing-gown when he's had a bath. Um, he's just a bit an-
  noyed at the moment. One of the — elves — shot him with an arrow.
Magrat But they do that to control people!
Ponder Um, he's not a person.
Librarian Oook!
Ponder Genetically, I mean.
Magrat Did they do that to you?
Ponder We've run into —
Librarian Ook.
Ponder — over elves a few times. But this is when the Librarian hit me.

The Bursar enters rather drunkenly

Librarian Oook.
Ponder Thank goodness. Knocked me cold. Otherwise I'd be like the others.
Magrat What others?
Ponder I think there's definitely been a cross-continuum breakthrough,
  and I'm sure there's a difference in energy levels.
Magrat What others?
Ponder The Bursar. I think we may have overdone the dried frog pills
  a bit. How — are — you — doing — sir?
Bursar Why, I'll have a little of the roast weasel, if you would be so good
  ... Call again tomorrow, baker, and we'll have a crusty one!
Magrat Now tell me what happened. Paying particular attention to what
  happened to the others.
Ponder Well — we all went to see this Entertainment, you see. A play.
  And it was very funny. There were all these yokels in their big boots
  and everything clumping around pretending to be lords and ladies.
  It was very funny. The Bursar laughed at them a lot. Mind you, he's
  been laughing at trees and rocks, too. And then — then there was this
  bit I can't really remember. It was something to do with the acting, I
  think. I mean, suddenly — it all seemed real. Everything round me just
  vanished, there was just the actors — and there was this hill ... I mean,
  they must have been good, because I really believed — and there was
  singing and it was wonderful and —
Librarian Oook.
Ponder Then the Librarian hit me.
Magrat Why?

Ponder Best if he tells it in his own words.
Librarian Oook, ook eek. Ook! Ook!
Bursar Cough, Julia! Over the Bender!
Magrat I don't understand what the Librarian said.
Ponder Um, we were all present at an interdimensional rip, caused by belief. The play was the last little thing that opened it up. There must have been a delicate area of instability very close. It's hard to explain, but if you had a rubber sheet and some lead weights I could demonstrate . .
Magrat You're trying to tell me those things exist because people believe in them?
Ponder Oh no. I imagine they exist anyway. They're here because people believe in them here.
Librarian Ook.
Ponder He ran off with us. They shot an arrow at him.
Librarian Eeek.
Ponder But it just made him itch.
Librarian Ook.
Ponder He can't abide elves. They smell wrong to him.
Magrat Yes, I expect they would. Dwarfs and trolls hate them, too. But I think they don't hate them as much as I do.
Ponder You can't fight them all. They're swarming like bees up there.
Magrat Did you see any witches at the Entertainment? You couldn't have missed them. There'd be a thin one glaring at everyone and a small fat one cracking nuts and laughing a lot. And they'd both have tall pointy hats.
Ponder Can't say I noticed them.
Magrat Then they couldn't have been there. Being noticed is what a witch is all about. I'm going on up there.
Ponder You'll need an army, miss.
Magrat But I haven't got an army. So I'm going to have to try by myself, aren't I?

Magrat exits

Ponder You know folk songs have got a lot to answer for.
Librarian Oook.
Ponder She's going to get utterly killed.
Librarian Oook.
Bursar Hallo, Mr Flowerpot, two pints of eels if you would be so good.
Ponder Anyone want to follow her?
Librarian Ook.
Bursar Whoops, there he goes with his big clock.
Ponder Was that a "yes"?
Librarian Oook.
Ponder Not yours, his.
Bursar Flobbly Wobbly, here comes our jelly.

Ponder I think that probably counts as a "yes."
Librarian Ook?
Bursar I've got a lovely new vest.
Ponder But look, the graveyards are full of people who rushed in bravely but unwisely.
Librarian Ook.
Bursar What'd he say?
Ponder I think he said "Sooner or later the graveyards are full of everybody." Oh, blast. Come on.
Bursar Yes indeedy, hands up the mittens, Mr Bosun!

The Bursar, Ponder and the Librarian exit

Black-out

Music plays

<h2 style="text-align:center">Scene 11</h2>

The Dancers

Two stones remain standing; the others have been knocked over and are strewn across the stage

The main stage is lit

The Queen of the Elves is on a throne with Verence next to her. His eyes are glazed. Granny stands between two Elves. The other Elves lounge about. During the scene the Elves reflect the Queen's emotions; when she is "winning" they laugh and smile; when she is angry they hiss and raise their weapons etc.

The music fades

Queen What is happening, old woman?
Granny It ain't easy is it? Thought it would be easy, didn't you?
Queen You've done some magic, haven't you?
Granny No magic. It's just that you've been away too long. Things change. The land belongs to humans now.
Queen That can't be the case. Humans take. They plough with iron. They ravage the land.
Granny Some do. I'll grant you that. Others put back more'n they take. They put back love. They tell the land what it is. Without humans Lancre'd

just be a bit of ground with green bits on it. We're all down here together, madam — us and the land. Every time people put a plough in the soil or planted a seed they took the land further away from you. Things change.

Queen But when we are married the land must accept me. By your own rules. I know how it works. The King and the land are one. The King and the Queen are one. And I shall be the Queen. What you shall be is something I have yet to decide ... And now someone comes with armour that doesn't fit and a sword she cannot use and an axe she can hardly even lift, because it is so romantic, is it not? What is her name?

Granny Magrat Garlick.

Queen She is a mighty enchantress, is she?

Granny She's good with herbs.

Queen I could kill her from here.

Granny Yes, but that wouldn't be much fun, would it? Humiliation is the key.

Queen You know, you think very much like an elf. It must be terrible, knowing that you have no friends. That no-one will care when you die. That you never touched a heart.

Granny Yes.

Queen And I'm sure you think about it — in those long evenings when there's no company but the ticking of the clock and the coldness of the room and you open the box and look at ...

Granny moves forward, trying to reach the Queen; the Elves stop her

Don't kill her. She is much more fun alive.

Magrat enters with an axe

Ah, the brave girl, come to save her fiancé, all alone? How sweet. Someone kill her.

An elf raises its sword but falls to the ground

Shawn Ogg and all the guests, Morris Men and Wizards, Nanny and Casanunda, run on, in a ramshackle attempt to be an army

What do you think, Esme Weatherwax? A valiant last stand? It's so beautiful, isn't it? I love the way humans think. They think like songs.

Magrat You get down off that throne!

The Queen advances on Magrat and smiles. Magrat half-raises her axe but slumps in the face of glamour. The army is transfixed

Granny Don't touch her.

Queen You can resist. But you see, it doesn't matter. We can take Lancre without a fight. Look at the brave army, standing there like sheep. Humans are so enthusiastic.

Granny You can't rule while I'm alive.

Queen There's no trickery here. No silly women with bags of sweets.

Granny You noticed that, did you? Gytha meant well, I expect. Daft old biddy. Mind if I sit down?

Queen Of course you may. You are an old woman, now, after all.

Granny That's the thing about witchcraft. It doesn't keep you young, but you do stay old for longer. Whereas you, of course, do not age.

Queen Indeed we do not.

Granny But I suspect you may be capable of being reduced. You meddled in a play. I believe you don't realize what you've done. Plays and books — you've got to keep an eye on the buggers. They'll turn on you. I mean to see that they do. Ain't that so, Fairy Peaseblossom?

Queen But that is not his name.

Granny We shall see. There's a lot more humans these days, and lots of them live in cities. And they've got iron in their heads. You're too late.

Queen No. Humans always need us.

Granny They don't. Sometimes they want you. But all you can give 'em is gold that melts away in the morning.

Queen There are those who would say that gold for one night is enough. Better than iron, you stupid old hag, you stupid child who has grown older and done nothing and been nothing.

Granny No. It's just soft and shiny. Pretty to look at and no damn use at all. But this is the real world, madam. That's what I had to learn. And real people in it. You got no right to 'em. People've got enough to cope with just being people. They don't need you swanking around with your shiny hair and eyes and shiny gold, going sideways through life, always young, always singing, never learning. I ain't having elves here. You make us want what we can't have and what you give us is worth nothing and what you take is everything and all there is left for us is the cold hillside and emptiness, and the laughter of the elves. So — (*pause*) bugger off.

Queen Make us, old woman.

A mental battle begins

Granny Madam? There ain't any rules are there?

Queen Rules? What are rules?

Granny I thought so. Gytha Ogg?

Nanny Yes, Esme?

Granny My box. You know. The one in the dresser. You'll know what to do.

Queen (*swaying*) You have learned.

Granny Oh, yes. You know I never entered your circle. I could see where it led. So I had to learn. All my life. The hard way. From the trolls and the dwarfs and from people. Even from pebbles.

Queen You will not be killed. I promise you that. You'll be left alive, to dribble and gibber and soil yourself and wander from door to door for scraps. And they'll say "there goes the mad woman."

Granny They say that now. They think I can't hear.

Queen But inside, inside I'll keep just a part of you which looks out through your eyes and knows what you've become ... And there will be none to help. No charity for the mad, old woman. And we'll be with you all the time inside your head, just to remind you. You could have been the great one, there was so much you could have done. And inside you'll know it, and you'll plead all the dark night long for the silence of the elves.

Granny slaps the Queen

Granny You threaten me with that? Me? Who am becoming old?

The Elves raise their bows, waiting for an order

Go back. You call yourself some kind of goddess and you know nothing, madam, nothing. What don't die can't live. What don't live can't change. What don't change can't learn. The smallest creature that dies in the grass knows more than you. You're right. I'm older. You've lived longer than me but I'm older than you. And better'n you. And, madam, that ain't hard.

The Queen raises her hand. Nanny Ogg falls to her knees

A good one. But still I stand, and still I'll not kneel.

Queen Oh, and I have no time for this. (*She gestures to her archers to shoot*)

The archers do not move

Granny They can't fire.

Queen You can't be holding them! You have not that much power!

Granny Do you want to find out how much power I have madam? Here, on the grass of Lancre?

Granny slaps the Queen again

What's this? Can't you resist me? Where's your power now, madam? Gather your power!

Queen You foolish old crone!
Granny (*dropping to her knees*) No ...

We hear the sound of a swarm of bees and an echo of the sinister sound heard earlier; over them, the following voice-over:

Granny (*V/O*) If only I could do it with bees. Hives notice changes in the land.
Nanny (*V/O*) You daft old besom, Esme. You know no-one's been able to do it with bees.
Ridcully (*V/O*) Trousers of Time. One of you goes down one leg, one of you goes down the other.
Granny (*V/O*) I think I've got it sorted.
Magrat (*V/O*) Are you all right, Granny?
Nanny (*V/O*) Esme?
Granny (*falling to the floor, screaming*) NO!
Queen Oh, but yes.

The Lights dim, the bee-swarm sound fills the auditorium and a lighting effect indicates that Granny is covered in bees

Granny (*to Magrat*) You want to be Queen?

Magrat raises her axe and swings it at the Queen. The Queen grabs Magrat's wrist, stopping the blow

Queen Oh yes. Really? You think so?

Magrat drops the axe

And you wanted to be a witch? The old witch is finished. I won't say she wasn't good. But she wasn't good enough. And you certainly aren't. Why don't you try some magic?

Magrat kicks the Queen and knocks her to the ground

Magrat Why, you're nothing. It's all in the mind, isn't it? Without glamour, you're ——
Queen Iron.

A mental battle. Then Magrat punches the Queen, who screams. They fight. Magrat picks up her axe and raises it. There is a silence

The sound of heavy footsteps is heard, approaching

The Long Man enters via the central door

Nanny He's back.
Ridcully (*raising his crossbow*) Will you look at the horns on that thing?
Nanny Put it down. It'd go right through him. He's not really here. He can't get past the doorway. But he can send his thoughts.

The Long Man walks towards the Queen and holds out a hand. She snarls at him

The Long Man Ill-met by moonlight, proud Titania.

Black-out

The Queen, the Long Man and all the Elves exit

The Lights come up

Nanny The first thing we do is put back the stones.
Magrat (*looking at Granny Weatherwax*) The second thing.
Nanny You did well there, girl. Didn't think you had it in you to survive an attack like that. It fairly had me widdling myself.
Magrat I've had practice.
Nanny Wake up, Esme. Well done. We won.
Ridcully Esme?
Nanny It must have taken it out of her, all that effort. Freeing Magrat and everything …
Ridcully She's dead.

Black-out

SCENE 12

Lancre Castle

The main stage and balcony are lit

In a dim light, Granny is lying on the table on the main stage, as did Diamanda earlier. She is being attended by Ridcully, who sits beside her, placing candles around her and putting lilies in her hands

Magrat and Nanny are on the balcony opening Granny's box, which is full of letters. They are both drinking tea

Magrat They're all old letters to her.

Nanny Nothing odd about that. Anyone can get letters.

Magrat I never thought we'd be doing this. I never thought we'd be reading her will. I thought she'd keep on going for ever.

Nanny Well, there it is. Tempus fuggit.

Magrat Nanny? I don't understand. She was your friend but you don't seem — well — upset?

Nanny Well, I've buried a few husbands and one or two kiddies. Anyway, if she hasn't gone to a better place she'll damn well be setting out to improve it.

Magrat Nanny?

Nanny Yes, love?

Magrat Did you know anything about the letter?

Nanny What letter?

Magrat The letter to Verence. He must have got it weeks before we got back.

Nanny Don't know anything about any letter to Verence.

Magrat Oh, hell. (*She holds up a letter*) I mean this letter. See?

Nanny (*reading*) Dear Sire, This is to inform you that Magrat Garlick will be returning to Lancre on or about Blind Pig Tuesday. She is a wet hen but she is clean and has got good teeth. If you wishes to marry her, then start arranging matters without delay, because if you just propose and similar, she will lead you a dance because there is no-one like Magrat for getting in the way of her own life. She does not know her own mind. You are King and can do what you like. PS: I hear there is talk about making witches pay tax. No king of Lancre has tried this for many a year; you could profit from their example.

Magrat She arranged it all! I got back and it was all arranged …

Nanny What would you have done if nothing had been arranged?

Magrat Well, I would … I mean, if he had … I'd …

Nanny You'd be getting married today, would you?

Magrat Well, that depends on …

Nanny You want to, don't you?

Magrat Well, yes of course, but …

Nanny That's nice then.

Magrat Yes, but she pushed me on one side and shut me up in the castle and I got so wound up ...

Nanny You were so angry that you actually stood up to the Queen. The old Magrat wouldn't have done that, would she? Esme could always see the real thing.

Magrat But I hated her and hated her and now she's dead!

Nanny Yes dear. (*She opens up an envelope and finds an "I ATEN'T DEAD" sign*) Come on. We ain't got much time!
Magrat What's the matter?
Nanny Bring the sugar bowl! Come on!

Black-out

The Lights come up on Ridcully, sitting next to Granny, whose body is surrounded by lilies

Nanny and Magrat enter

Nanny What's all this?
Ridcully Well, it didn't seem right to leave her all alone …
Nanny Oh dear, oh dear. Candles and lilies. I bet you pinched 'em yourself, out of the garden. And then you all shut her away indoors like this. And no-one even thought to leave a damn window open! Can't you hear them?
Ridcully Hear what?

Nanny opens the door. We hear the sound of a swarm of bees

What did you …?
Nanny She's going to swank about this for weeks. No-one's ever done it with bees. Their minds everywhere, see? Not just one bee. In the whole swarm.

Granny sits up slowly and focuses on Nanny

Granny I wantzzz a bunzzch of flowerzz, a pot of honey, and someone to szzzting.
Nanny I brung the sugar bowl, Esme.
Granny I done it with beezz! No-one can do it with beezzz, and I done it! You endzz up with your mind all flying in different directionzzz! You got to be good to do it with beezzz!
Ridcully You're alive?
Granny That's what a univerzzity education doezz for you. You've only got to be sitting up and talking for five minutzz and they can work out you're alive.
Nanny I knew you wasn't certain!
Granny Czertain? Of course I waz certain! Never in any doubt whatsoever.
Magrat You never had a moment's doubt?
Granny What's been happening while I've been away?
Nanny Well. Magrat stood up to the ——
Granny Oh, I knew she'd do that. Had the wedding, have you?

Magrat Of course not! Brother Perdore of the Nine Day Wonderers was going to do it and he was knocked out cold by an elf, and anyway people are all ——

Granny Don't let's have any excuses. Anyway, a senior wizard can conduct a service at a pinch, ain't that right?

Ridcully I — I — I think so.

Granny Right. A wizard's only a priest without a god and a damp handshake.

Magrat But half the guests have run away!

Granny We'll have to round up some more.

Magrat Mrs Scorbic will never get the wedding feast done in time!

Granny You'll have to tell her to.

Magrat I haven't got a dress!

Granny What's that you've got on? Looks good to me. Nanny'll do your hair.

Magrat I think I'll leave it.

Granny That's the way of it. It's not what you've got that matters, it's how you've got it.

Nanny Where's the groom?

Magrat He's a bit muzzy. Not sure what happened.

Nanny Perfectly normal after a stag night.

They all exit

There is the sound of the ringing of wedding bells

Black-out

SCENE 13

Lancre Castle

The balcony is lit

Magrat, Verence and their guests — Ponder, the Librarian, the Bursar and Casanunda — are on the balcony. Nanny and Granny are at stage level but are unlit as yet

Ponder I'm sure you'll be very happy.

Magrat
Verence } (*together*) Thank you.

Librarian Ook!

Magrat
Verence } (*together*) Thank you.

Bursar Nail it to the counter, Lord Ferguson, and damn the cheesemongers!

Magrat ⎫ (*together*) Thank you.
Verence ⎭

Casanunda May I kiss the bride?

Verence I'm sorry, you are … ?

Casanunda (*proffering his card*) My card.

Verence (*looking at the card*) Ah, uh. Um. Well, well. Number two, eh?

Casanunda I try harder.

Verence Could I have a word with you in a minute or two?

The Lights come up on the stage level

During the following, Mrs Scorbic and Millie Chillum join the others on the balcony. Millie carries Magrat's helmet and crossbow

Granny She'll be getting ideas above her station in life.

Nanny She's a queen. That's pretty high. Almost as high as witches.

Granny Yes — well — but you ain't got to give yourself airs. We're advantaged, yes, but we act with modesty and we don't Put Ourselves Forward. No-one could say I haven't been decently modest all my life.

Nanny You've always been a bit of a shy violet. I'm always telling people, when it comes to humility you won't find anyone more humile than Esme Weatherwax.

Granny I was talking, Gytha.

Nanny Sorry ... Funny to think of our Magrat being married and everything.

Granny What do you mean, everything?

Nanny Well, you know — married. I gave her a few tips. Always wear something in bed. Keeps a man interested.

Granny You always wore your hat.

Nanny Right. I like the way they give us all a bit o'the wedding cake in a little bag. You know, they says, if you put a bit under your pillow, you dream of your future husb …

Granny It's all right. I don't mind. Everything happens somewhere. So it's all the same in the end.

The Lights fade on the main stage

Magrat I thought perhaps some more salad and quiche and some light ——

Mrs Scorbic Them elves turned the whole kitchen upside down. It's going to take me days to get it straight. Anyway, everyone knows raw vegetables are bad for you, and I can't be having with them eggy pies.

Magrat But ...

Mrs Scorbic I'm not goin' to be ordered around by some chit of a girl.

Millie Chillum hands Magrat her helmet. Magrat swaps her crown for the helmet and takes the crossbow from Millie

Magrat Go ahead, bake my quiche.

The Lights come up on the main stage

Granny I thought Magrat was very surprised when you recited that poem — the one where you did the gestures.

Nanny Oh, that poem. I thought she looked happy, standing there wearing about half of a torn muddy dress and chain mail. Hey, d'you what she told me?

Granny What?

Nanny You know that ole painting of Queen Ynci? You know the one with the iron bodice, with all the spikes. Well, she said she was sure the — the spirit of Ynci was helping her. She said she wore the armour and she did things she'd never dare do.

Granny My word. So you didn't tell her that Queen Ynci never existed then?

Nanny No point.

Granny Funny thing, even when Magrat's completely different, she's just the same.

Casanunda and Ridcully come down from the balcony

Magrat, Verence and the guests exit during the following

Casanunda 'Allo, my little Rosebud.

Nanny Are you going to the dance?

Granny Are you?

Nanny Well — Mr Casanunda did ask if I could show him the Long Man. You know. Properly.

Casanunda Can't get enough of earthworks.

Granny Act your age, Gytha.

Nanny Don't have to act, can do it automatic. Acting half my age; now that's the difficult trick. Anyway you didn't answer me.

Granny Mr Ridcully and I are going to have a stroll.

Ridcully We are?

Nanny Oh, that's nice.

Granny Gytha Ogg, if you keep on looking at me like that I shall give you a right ding around the ear.

Nanny I expect you want to talk about old times.

Granny Maybe old times. Maybe other times.

Nanny and Casanunda exit

Granny and Ridcully, alone on stage now, walk up the steps to the bridge on the balcony

It all works out somewhere. Your young wizard knows that, he just puts daft words around it.

Ridcully Do you think that — somewhere — it all went right?

Granny Yes. Here! But there too.

Ridcully What?

Granny I mean that somewhere Mustrum Ridcully married Esmeralda Weatherwax and they lived — lived happily ever after. More or less. As much as anyone does.

Ridcully How d'you know?

Granny I've been picking up lots of her memories. She seemed happy enough. And I ain't easily pleased.

Ridcully How can you do that?

Granny I try to be good at everything I do.

Ridcully Did she say anything about ——

Granny She didn't say nothing! She don't even know we exist! Don't ask questions! It's enough to know that everything happens somewhere, isn't it?

Ridcully Is that the best you can tell me?

Granny It's the best there is. Or the next best.

Music plays

FURNITURE AND PROPERTY LIST

ACT I

Prologue

On stage: Eight-stone circle

Off stage: Bugle (**Shawn**)

Scene 1

On stage: Eight-stone circle

Off stage: Three broomsticks (**Granny, Nanny, Magrat**)

Scene 2

Set: Small oven with iron kettle and teacups on it

Strike: Stone circle

Personal: **Granny Weatherwax**: "I ATEN'T DEAD" sign

Scene 3

Set: Small table with lit candle
Chalk circle of magical symbols
Tarot cards for Diamanda

Strike: Oven, kettle, teacups

Scene 4

Set: Screen

Strike: Small table, candle, chalk circle

Off stage: Large bundle of clothing, diagram

Scene 5

Set: Benches and chairs
              Towel, bucket, plate of oranges for Nanny

Strike: Screen

Personal: **Nanny Ogg**: bag of sweets, bottle of brandy

Scene 6

Set: Small oven with iron kettle and teacups on it

Strike: Benches and chairs

Off stage: Play scripts (**Jason** and **Rude Mechanicals**)

Scene 7

Strike: Oven, kettle, teacups

Off stage: Stepladder, crossbow (**Casanunda**)

Personal: **Ridcully**: cards, bag of money

Scene 8

Set: Eight-stone circle

During Black-out p. 23

Strike: Five stones

During Black-out p. 24

Re-set: Five stones

Off stage: Frying-pan (**Nanny**)

Personal: **Elves**: daggers
              Other elves: bows and arrows
              Nanny: penknife

Scene 9

Set: Long dining table
              Chairs
              Place settings for two, food etc.

Strike: Eight-stone circle

Off stage: Water, bandages etc. (**Magrat** and **Nanny**)
                Books, mouldy bread, blankets (**Shawn**)

Scene 10

Strike: Table and settings, chairs, all props

Set: Three stones

Off stage: Props, scripts, bundle, jugs of scumble (**Rude Mechanicals**)

Personal: **Elves**: knives

ACT II

Scene 1

Set: Eight-stone circle

Scene 2

Strike: Eight-stone circle

Off stage: Mail sack containing letters and parcels, some containing books
                (**Wizards**)
                Several iron objects, some wrapped in cloth (**Shawn**)

Personal: **Magrat**: fan

Scene 3

Set: Food and drink for **Mr Spriggins** and **Servants**

Strike: All props from Scene 2

Off stage: Sign saying "Coaches to the Entertainment" (**Shawn Ogg**)

Scene 4

No props

SCENE 5

Off stage: Bag of peanuts (**Librarian**)
Bag (**Magrat**)

During black-out p.48

Set: Portrait of Queen Ynci

SCENE 6

Strike: Portrait of Queen Ynci

Off stage: Bows and arrows (**Elves**)

SCENE 7

Set: Portrait of Queen Ynci

Personal: **Elf 3**: crossbow bolt
Elf 4: knife

SCENE 8

Strike: Portrait of Queen Ynci

Set: Some of the stones; not all standing
Sack containing bells, sticks, buckets and accordion for **Carter**

SCENE 9

Set: Standing stone at top of ladder, featuring man painted in white

Re-set: Two stones at bottom of ladder

Strike: All other stones

SCENE 10

Strike: Stones

Off stage: Crossbow and axe (**Magrat**)
Bows and arrows (**Elves**)

Scene 11

Set: Two stones standing; others strewn across stage

Off stage: Axe (**Magrat**)

Scene 12

Set: On Main Stage: Table
                  Candles
                  Lilies for **Ridcully**

                  On Balcony: **Granny**'s box containing letters
                  Teacups

Strike: Stones

Scene 13

Strike: All props from Scene 12

Off stage: Helmet and crossbow (**Millie**)

LIGHTING PLOT

ACT I, Prologue

To open: Darkness

Cue 1	Refrain of "elf music" *Bring up lights on stone circle*	(Page 1)

Cue 2	**Elves**: "They beget terror." *Bring up lights on whole stage*	(Page 1)

Cue 3	**Queen**: "Step through!" *Black-out*	(Page 2)

Cue 4	**King Verence** enters on to the balcony *Bring up lights on balcony*	(Page 2)

Cue 5	**Verence**: "The old rose garden." *Cross-fade lights from balcony to Dancers*	(Page 4)

Cue 6	Music *Black-out*	(Page 4)

ACT I, Scene 1

To open: General exterior light on main stage area

Cue 7	**Granny** exits *Black-out*	(Page 7)

ACT I, Scene 2

To open: General interior light on main stage area

Cue 8	**Granny**: "I wasn't feeling well." *Black-out*	(Page 9)

ACT I, Scene 3

To open: General interior light on main stage area with covering spot for candle

Cue 9	**Granny**: "You didn't see us in." *Black-out*	(Page 11)

ACT I, Scene 4

To open: General interior light on main stage area

Cue 10   **Magrat**: "And don't you forget it."   (Page 13)
             Black-out

ACT I, Scene 5

To open: General exterior light on main stage area

Cue 11   **Nanny**: "… on Midsummer Eve."   (Page 17)
             Black-out

ACT I, Scene 6

To open: General interior light on main stage area

Cue 12   **Obidiah**: "Where no-one goes."   (Page 19)
             Black-out

ACT I, Scene 7

To open: General exterior light on main stage area

Cue 13   **Ridcully**: "What a bastard."   (Page 21)
             Black-out

ACT I, Scene 8

To open: General exterior light on main stage area

Cue 14   Noise of metal being torn away   (Page 23)
             Lights flicker; then black-out

Cue 15   **Queen** and **followers** enter   (Page 23)
             Bring up lights on main stage area

Cue 16   Magical sound effect   (Page 24)
             Lights flicker; black-out

Cue 17   **Nanny** hides behind a stone: when ready   (Page 80)
             Bring up general exterior lights on main stage area

Cue 18   **Granny**, **Nanny** and **Diamanda** exit   (Page 25)
             Black-out

ACT I, Scene 9

To open: General interior light on main stage area

Cue 19	**Magrat** and **Verence** exit	(Page 30)
	Black-out	

ACT I, Scene 10

To open: General exterior light on main stage area

Cue 20	The **Wizards** exit	(Page 32)
	Black-out	

ACT I, Scene 11

To open: General exterior light on main stage area

Cue 21	Sinister sound effect	(Page 35)
	Black-out	
Cue 22	**Jason** falls asleep	(Page 35)
	Dim lights; red wash from stone circle	

ACT II

ACT II, Scene 1

To open: General exterior light on main stage area

Cue 23	**Jason**: " … to see what century it is."	(Page 36)
	Black-out	

ACT II, Scene 2

To open: General exterior light on main stage area and balcony

Cue 24	**Shawn**: " … to do the trumpet, I know that."	(Page 40)
	Black-out	

ACT II, Scene 3

To open: General interior light on main stage area

Cue 25	Pyrotechnic explosion	(Page 42)
	Black-out	

Cue 26   **Nanny** and **Verence** take up positions by the door   (Page 42)
        Bring up lights on main stage area

Cue 27   **Casanunda**: " … special arrangements."   (Page 44)
        Black-out

ACT II, Scene 4

To open: General exterior light on balcony

Cue 28   Music   (Page 45)
        Black-out

ACT II, Scene 5

To open: General interior light on balcony

Cue 29   **Librarian**: "Oook? Oook?"   (Page 46)
        Bring up lights on main stage

Cue 30   **Elves** follow **Magrat** off   (Page 48)
        Black-out

Cue 31   Portrait of Queen Ynci is placed on stage   (Page 48)
        Bring up lights on main stage

Cue 32   **Magrat** exits   (Page 48)
        Black-out

ACT II, Scene 6

To open: General exterior light on entire stage

Cue 33   **Ridcully**: "Right! I'll be back instantly."   (Page 50)
        Flash of light then black-out

Cue 34   **Ridcully** exits   (Page 50)
        Bring up lights on entire stage

Cue 35   **Granny**: "All of me."   (Page 50)
        Black-out

ACT II, Scene 7

To open: General interior light on main stage

Cue 36   **Shawn**: "Good luck!"   (Page 53)
        Black-out

Lighting Plot   83

ACT II, SCENE 8

To open: General exterior light on main stage

Cue 37   They dance off the stage   (Page 55)
             Black-out

ACT II, SCENE 9

To open: General interior light on main stage and balcony

Cue 38   **Casanunda**: " … like your picture."   (Page 58)
             Black-out

ACT II, SCENE 10

To open: General exterior light on main stage

Cue 39   **The Bursar, Ponder** and the **Librarian** exit   (Page 62)
             Black-out

ACT II, SCENE 11

To open: General exterior light on main stage

Cue 40   **Queen** (V/O): "Oh, but yes."   (Page 66)
             Dim lights

Cue 41   Bee sound fills auditorium   (Page 66)
             Lighting effect indicates **Granny** *is covered in bees*

Cue 42   **The Long Man**: "… proud Titania."   (Page 67)
             Black-out

Cue 43   **Queen, Long Man** and **Elves** exit   (Page 67)
             Bring up lights

Cue 44   **Ridcully**: "She's dead."   (Page 67)
             Black-out

ACT II, SCENE 12

To open: General interior light on main stage and balony; main stage lighting is
dim, with covering spot on candles

Cue 45   **Nanny**: "Bring the sugar-bowl! Come on!"   (Page 69)
             Black-out on balcony; brighten lights on main stage

Cue 46   Ringing of wedding bells   (Page 70)
                Black-out

ACT II, Scene 13

To open: General interior lighting on balcony

Cue 47   **Verence**: "… in a minute or two?"   (Page 71)
                Bring up lights on main stage

Cue 48   **Granny**: "… all the same in the end."   (Page 71)
                Fade lights on main stage

Cue 49   **Magrat**: "Go ahead, bake my quiche."   (Page 72)
                Bring up lights on main stage

EFFECTS PLOT

ACT I

Cue 1   When play begins   (Page 1)
          Low thrum; refrain of "elf music"

Cue 2   **Queen**: "Soon."   (Page 4)
          Music; excerpt from "Long Lankin"

Cue 3   SCENE 1 begins; when ready   (Page 4)
          Fade music

Cue 4   **Granny**: "How about noon?"   (Page 11)
          "Man With No Name" music

Cue 5   As SCENE 5 begins   (Page 13)
          Music: "Eye of the Tiger"

Cue 6   **Granny**: "Of course. Someone's got to."   (Page 14)
          Sound effect indicating sinister presence

Cue 7   Black-out   (Page 17)
          "Twilight Zone" music

Cue 8   SCENE 6 begins; when ready   (Page 18)
          Fade music

Cue 9   **Ridcully** points his fingers   (Page 20)
          *Pyrotechnic explosion to **Casanunda**'s L*

Cue 10   **Granny** runs into the circle   (Page 23)
          Magical sound effect and sound of metal being torn away

Cue 11   **Granny** runs into the circle with **Diamanda**   (Page 24)
          Magical sound effect

Cue 12   **Granny**, **Nanny** and **Diamanda** exit   (Page 25)
          Music: "Never Wed an Old Man"

Cue 13   As SCENE 9 begins   (Page 25)
          Fade music

ACT II

CPSIA information can be obtained
at www.ICGtesting.com
Printed in the USA
BVHW060715200620
581890BV00006B/609

9 780573 018886